FOREWORD BY TODD H

VICTOR HUGO MANZANILLA

AWAKEN YOUR INNER HERO

7 STEPS TO A SUCCESSFUL AND MEANINGFUL LIFE

GRUPO NELSON
Una división de Thomas Nelson Publishers
Desde 1798

NASHVILLE   MÉXICO DF.   RÍO DE JANEIRO

Awaken Your Inner Hero

© 2017 by Victor Hugo Manzanilla
Published in Nashville, Tennessee, United States of America.
Grupo Nelson is a registered trademark of Thomas Nelson.
www.gruponelson.com

Title in Spanish: *Despierta tu héroe interior*
© 2015 by Victor Hugo Manzanilla
Published by Grupo Nelson, a registered trademark of Thomas Nelson.

Editor-in-Chief: *Graciela Lelli*

ISBN: 978-0-71809-841-4

Printed in the United States of America

17 18 19 20 21 DCI 9 8 7 6 5 4 3 2 1

CONTENTS

PART FOUR: RESURRECTION

PART FIVE: MY ADVICE FOR YOUR JOURNEY

PART SIX: FINAL WORDS

To My Son Benjamin:

Some day you will be able to read these pages. My greatest desire is that they help you overcome any fear you have and that they inspire you to set out to live a life of unique adventure.

You are the hero of your story. Sing your song at the top of your lungs; the world needs to hear it. I can't wait to see what God has in store for you.

I love you forever.

Download the

"**Awaken**

Your

Inner Hero"

free study at:

www.innerheroguide.com

FOREWORD

YOU FRIEND HAVE BEEN GIVEN a tremendous gift.

By virtue of the fact that you are alive, here and now, with the ability to hold this book and process its ideas, you are among the top fraction of a percent of all beings who have ever graced this planet in terms of opportunity. There are people throughout all of known history who would have traded anything to simply live one of your "normal" days. Even the least wealthy among us would have been considered wildly advantaged just a few centuries ago.

So, in the words of the poet Mary Oliver, "Tell me, what is it you plan to do with your one wild and precious life?"

I believe that how you answer this question defines everything about you. If you choose—by design or default—to simply move through your life reacting to your circumstances by taking the predictable path, chasing comfort, and trying to make as few waves as possible then your life will likely be fine. Just fine. And frankly, if that's what you're aiming for, there's nothing wrong with that. You'll probably hit your target.

However—and I promise you this—you will always wonder "what if?" What if I had taken that chance? What if I'd introduced myself to her or him? What if I'd actually tried? Though you lived your life, it was never actually yours.

On the other hand, if you choose to take the wise advice of Victor Hugo Manzanilla and treat your life as a journey to be embraced and an adventure to be relished, your life will be full of highs and lows, successes and failures, joys and heartaches. There will be times when you wonder if it was all worth it. But, the one thing I promise you is this: your life will be yours, and no one else's. You will go to your grave knowing that you lived your days to their fullest, and that you squeezed every last ounce of beauty and wonder out of them while you had the chance.

So, what will you do with your one and only life? Will you choose to be the hero of your story or a background character in your own plot line?

Today is your day of reckoning, and Victor Hugo Manzanilla is your guide. This book is full of such practical wisdom that it's impossible to read it without being moved and transformed. Live The Hero's Journey, embrace your call, and bring your gift to the world. We need you to live your life. Will you?

Todd Henry
September, 2016

INTRODUCTION

I WANT TO TELL YOU A STORY that changed my life and will surely change yours as well.

It all began on a Sunday like any other. We had made it through a hellish winter—sometimes I don't know which is more infernal, the extreme heat or the winter cold in Ohio— that brutalizes us five months of the year here in the North, and we were slowly beginning to see blue skies and hear the birds sing again.

After church service we greeted our friends Dave and Beth as we normally did.

Dave and Beth are a couple that became close friends when I moved from Venezuela to Cincinnati. If you have ever emigrated, you know what it is means to leave your people, your city, and your country as a somebody and overnight become a nobody. Dave and Beth were that couple that began to make us feel like we were somebodies once again.

Dave is the type of person who always has new ideas. His mind never stops working. Each week, without fail, he comes to me with a new project, adventure, or business idea.

And he doesn't stop talking. It's as if his soul refuses to be tamed by a common life, routine, or even the impossible. He is always thinking about something new that might be achieved.

That day, I was met with an invitation:

"Would you like to go meet Donald Miller?"

"Who is Donald Miller?" I asked.

"Don," as he is called, "is a famous writer," Dave said. "He wrote a book called *Blue Like Jazz* that was hugely successful that I absolutely loved. Don is here in Cincinnati today speaking about his next book, and I would really like to meet him."

I never liked these last-minute invitations. For some reason I always felt they messed up my already well-planned day. It was as if my appointment book was always making me refuse the call to something new, to something unknown.

The truth is that refusing something new was very common for me. The appointment book was just an excuse.

That day was like any other Sunday. Nevertheless, going to see Don meant a drastic change from what I had in mind. I would have to forfeit going out to eat at the place we normally did on Sundays, and I would miss out on the usual Sunday meal, and the same cup of coffee that I ordered every Sunday. Oh, and, of course, I would risk not getting home in time to see *Extreme Makeover: Home Edition*, a program where homes are rebuilt for the poor or someone going through difficult circumstances. I watched it faithfully every Sunday. I would cry at the end when the remodeled house was turned over to its owner and would feel that I had somehow contributed to the good of humanity.

I don't know why it makes you feel so good. It's like a low-cost way of imparting some benevolence to the world. We watch a video or see some story of kindness, compassion, or redemption and it touches our hearts. We share it on social media, and we feel like we are part of that story when in reality we have done nothing. And, we do nothing differently from that moment. It's as though the act of watching something, crying a little, and sharing in the stories lend a bit of significance to our lives. As if that were the only way we could get involved and be a part of a great story.

So, going back to Dave's invitation, for some reason that I still don't understand, that day I decided not to eat the same meal I ate every Sunday in the same restaurant with the same cup of coffee I always had, or watch my favorite Sunday program so I could go with Dave to meet Don.

That day something happened inside of me that was a turning point in my life. Don planted a seed in my heart that led me to change; a seed that, years later, sprouted and became this book.

I want to be honest with you. I wrote this book with the goal of helping you to change your life for the better. This is not a book meant to simply entertain you, but rather a book that will touch the deepest fibers of your being with a clear search for change.

If this book does not lead you to make changes in your life, then I have failed. It's that simple.

This book will get in your face but it will also throw an arm around you. It will discuss profound topics and at the same time make you laugh over trivialities. One moment we will be discussing philosophical issues about life, suffering, and its purpose, and the next we will explore the realm of the practical and pragmatic and how to make them a reality in your life. I will tell you stories that you have never heard before, and all of them will have one clear objective: to move you to action.

> If this book does not lead you to make changes in your life, then I have failed. It's that simple.
> #innerherobook.com

My hope is that one day when I am listening to your story that you will mention, although it may be subtly, that this book inspired, motivated, or revealed something to you that brought you to that place of change.

If in some way this book helps someone who has given up singing decide he wants to sing again; or someone who is at the point of ending his marriage to hold on a little longer; or someone who has forgotten his dreams to reconsider them and begin to walk them out; or someone who has lived a lackluster life to find their purpose and return to a life filled with passion—if this book helps you develop a better life story, then I will have achieved my goal.

> **If this book helps you develop a better life story, then I will have achieved my goal. #innerherobook.com**

...So, I got in the car with Dave who the entire trip never stopped talking about one idea or another while we were on the way to see Don.

So what happened that day that changed my life? Welcome to the journey that will change yours as well.

PART ONE

QUIET DESPERATION

CHAPTER 1

QUIET DESPERATION

WE ARRIVED A FEW MINUTES LATE for Don's presentation. I was relieved when we entered the theater and realized that Don had not yet begun.

One thing you should understand is that I didn't know who Don was. I was in a theater full of admirers of his books and his talks, but I didn't know what to expect. I had no clue.

Don told us his story, a story that raised a question that changed my life.

Don was a writer who had already published several books to a certain amount of success when suddenly his book *Blue Like Jazz*, published the previous year as a memoir, hit the best-sellers lists.

Without expecting it, Don had become one of the most successful authors in the country.

Sometime later, Don received an unexpected call. A couple of Hollywood directors wanted to make a movie about his life.

Faced with the tempting offer, Don accepted and began meeting with the directors to prepare for the project.

The directors were already well into the process of working on the creation of the scripts and the storyline when Don began to realize that they were changing certain details of his life. At first, because they were small details, he didn't think too much about it, but when they began to make significant changes, Don decided to speak up:

"I mean no disrespect," he said. "But what is wrong with the Don in the book?" Don asked the directors.

The first director sat thoughtfully and collected his ideas. He scratched his chin and collected some sympathy. "In a pure story," he said like a professor, "there is a purpose in every scene, in every line of dialogue. A movie is *going* somewhere."

That last line rang in my ear like an accusation. I felt defensive, as though the scenes in my life weren't going anywhere. I mean, I knew they weren't going anywhere...

"What he is trying to say," the second director said, reaching for a jar of olives, "is that your real life is boring."

"Boring?" I blurted.

"Boring," he repeated.[1]

At that moment I could hear hundreds of laughs in the auditorium. Don is a funny guy, and throughout his presentation there were plenty of things to laugh at, but not this one. At least, not for me.

The laughter from the audience plunged a dagger straight through me. For a few seconds that seemed like hours, a film of my life played out in my mind. A life full of routine—the same places, the same foods, the same Mondays through Fridays, the same weekends, the same route to the office every day, the same floor, the same desk, the same old predictable plans. So much sameness.

Was my life boring?

If I were to receive a call from some Hollywood directors proposing to make a movie of my life, would it be the kind that captivates audiences, full of risk, adventure, and victory? Or would it be one of those movies where people get up and walk out halfway through?

Would a movie about my life inspire others? For a second I was a bit less ambitious.

Would a movie about my life at least inspire my family? Would my wife, my son, my parents, and my closest friends be positively impacted by the story of my life? Or would they simply go see the movie as a favor to a friend in the same way that we go to their children's weddings or graduation ceremonies that seem to drag on forever when we're invited?

At that moment, I knew the answer. It wasn't that I hadn't accomplished great things, or that I spent the entire day on the couch watching infomercials, but there was something within me that confronted me with the reality that I was not living my life to its maximum, that I had somehow made myself a prisoner of comfort, routine, and security. That the passion I once had for the unknown, that inexplicable union of both fear and excitement of undertaking an adventure for the first time, had been snuffed out.

Which brings me to my second question. Is your life boring?

I don't want you to misunderstand the question. I'm not saying that you haven't achieved great things or lived remarkable moments with the people you love. And, I'm not saying that you don't have people who admire you and whom you have impacted in a positive way. It's simply a question that requires a very personal response. It's a much deeper question, one that is meant to go straight to your heart. Do you feel you're living your life to its maximum?

Do you feel that when you search the depths of your heart that you have lived your life to its fullest, without any regrets? Have you given your all to go after your dreams—each and every day?

If some Hollywood directors were to call you and ask to make a movie of your life, what would it be like?

"Most men lead lives of quiet desperation and go to the grave

> Most men lead lives of quiet desperation and go to the grave with the song still in them.
> #innerherobook.com

with the song still in them,"[2] This is the kind of profound statement around which an entire book could be written.

> Too many people live lives like these, ones of quiet desperation. We sense an emptiness in our hearts. #innerherobook.com

Too many people live lives like these, ones of quiet desperation. We sense an emptiness in our hearts. The life that we once dreamed of no longer exists, or maybe it never existed.

As we grew, perhaps because of the expectations of others, life's problems or complications, traumas, or lack of guidance and wisdom, we began letting those dreams and desires for adventure, risk, and victory die out.

Without realizing it, many of us ended up in jobs that don't fulfill us, living lives of routine, with the same places, the same meals, the same Mondays through Fridays, the same weekends, the same routes to the office, the same floor, the same desk, the same predictable plans, and an infinity of other sames. It's like a trap that we built for ourselves little by little. Only now we don't even realize that we're trapped. The trap transformed itself into our real world, and we became so accustomed to it that it became our new home.

Is it possible to live life to its fullest? To come to the end of our lives having sung our own song at the top of our lungs every day of our existence?

That day in the theater, Don spoke for several hours. And, though I don't remember too terribly much of what was said after my life played out in my head and I sat pondering what to do about it, something I did catch and hold onto was his point on universal principles.

Universal principles are the tools that writers, poets, and filmmakers use to build great stories around. Stories that move us and we connect to. Such stories attract thousands of people who immerse themselves in a narrative of heroes with a calling, of lives with purpose.

The thing that attracts me to universal principles is that they are invariable. If they work in movies and novels to develop a focused story line, they will work as we apply them to our real lives as well. Which brings me to the following conclusion. If we can understand the art and science behind stories, why some stories are successful and touch our hearts while others are boring and quickly forgotten, then we can apply those same principles to our lives to achieve a life worth living, a life story worth telling.

We will live a life in which we will sing our song at the right time. And we will come to the end of our days having given it our all, with no regrets: a life lived to the maximum.

> If we can understand the art and science behind stories, then we can apply these same principles to our lives to achieve a story worth living, a life story worth telling. #innerherobook.com

CHAPTER 2

GREAT STORIES

IN 1997, JAMES CAMERON BROUGHT the public a movie that quickly became the most successful film of its time. With an investment of a little over two hundred million dollars, *Titanic* was released to the public and earned over two billion dollars.

Titanic is the first film in history to gross more than a billion dollars. I remember going to the theater to see it not once, not twice, but three times. That movie was a sensation like none other.

What is interesting is that it's a movie based on history. Everyone who went to see the movie knew how it would end. They knew the boat was going to sink. I mean, I imagine when you saw it, you never expected the ship to somehow manage to avoid the iceberg and reach dry land.

How is it possible that a film in which everyone already knows how the ending will turn out can be so successful? Why did so many people go to see the movie again and again when they knew exactly what was going to happen?

The truth is that *Titanic* is not a story about the sinking of a ship; it's a story of what happens in the midst of tragedy. It's not even a love story between Jack and Rose. *Titanic* is a story about freedom. Rose's freedom.

This is why we connect with the film: because of the theme of freedom.

The film begins with a young girl named Rose who is forced to live a life she does not want to live, to marry a man she is not in love with in order to secure the financial future of a family who is on the brink of bankruptcy.

In the midst of her desperation, Jack appears. He is a poor young man passionate about living life to the fullest, a young man with freedom. They meet, fall in love, and begin living a life of new adventures that change their lives forever.

Rose, accustomed to wealth and privilege, begins to realize that she is not truly free. Meanwhile, Jack who has no money but is filled with a spirit of adventure, is living a life of true freedom.

Though their love story only lasts a few days, it is one of intensity. But, the results of that experience transform Rose's future. She is brought back to life, a life that has escaped death (and I am not referring to her physical death).

There is a scene at the end of the film in which we are uncertain if Rose, now an old woman, is sleeping or lying on her deathbed. The camera pans to photos on her bedside table showing us the most treasured moments of her life. We see Rose preparing to fly a plane, riding a horse, surrounded by a family, graduating from university. We behold a happy Rose—a Rose who has lived her life as she chose to live it.

In short, meeting Jack had saved Rose.

The movie *Titanic* is not about a ship. The sinking of the ship is simply a platform upon which an even more profound story, a story that connects with us on a deeper level, is presented.

Ten years later, *Poseidon*, another movie about a shipwreck was released. It had a budget similar to that of *Titanic* but had access to much better technology, including special effects that it uses liberally throughout the film to tell its tale. However, the results were disappointing. *Poseidon* only grossed 180 million dollars—eleven times less than the two *billion* dollars *Titanic* made.

How can you have two similar films, with similar budgets, with nearly similar technology, but end up with such a disparity in popularity and earnings?

The difference is the story. While *Poseidon* focuses on the story of a disaster of a ship using incredible special effects, *Titanic* focuses on a more powerful story, the story of the freedom of its main character.

This brings me to the following conclusion. Two people can have the same resources, the same education, even come from the same family, but the way they define and live out their lives will make the biggest difference.

How do you want to live out your life story? How do you want to be remembered?

This question moved an entire Scottish army to fight for their freedom against the yoke of English oppression in the thirteenth century. *Braveheart*[1] tells of Scotsman William Wallace who steps up to lead the fight for the freedom of his homeland.

Edward Longshanks rules as one of the worst and most tyrannical kings Scotland has seen. Scottish nobility whose duty it is to protect their people have made secret treaties with the English in order to protect their wealth and status. Under Longshanks, Scottish women are raped and thousands of Scotsmen are killed.

It's under these circumstances that William Wallace enters the scene, the first Scottish warrior to take on King Edward Longshanks of England. Reacting in indignation, the king sends a large attachment of English soldiers to the area of Stirling to destroy the rebels once and for all.

Two people can have the same resources, the same education, even come from the same family, but the way they define and live out their lives will make the biggest difference. #innerherobook.com

Thousands of Scotsmen descend upon the battlefield, ready to begin the confrontation. Scottish leaders, lead largely by its cowardly nobles, wish to avoid the battle. Claiming unfairness in size of the two armies as an excuse not to fight, the Scottish noblemen decide to negotiate. These leaders know a successful negotiation will bring them more power and land.

Likewise, the Scots, upon seeing the size of the English army and observing their leaders attempting to negotiate a deal, lose heart and begin to leave the battlefield. One by one, then group after group begins to flee.

William Wallace, seeing his countrymen deserting the battlefield as negotiations begin, stands before the remaining rebel army and gives one of the most powerful discourses I have ever heard.

After Wallace unsuccessfully commands them to hold the battle line, he reminds them that a life lived with no freedom is a life that isn't worth living. He tells them if they choose not to fight at that very moment, at the end of their lives, they will wish they had another opportunity like the moment they face to fight for their freedom although they might have to risk their lives to obtain it.

> Day after day, week after week, year after year thousands of people die regretting not having tried to accomplish all that they dreamed of doing.
>
> #innerherobook.com

The speech motivates the Scottish army to stay on the battlefield, fight, and win.

So let me ask the question again. How do you want to live out your life story? How do you want to be remembered?

Day after day, week after week, year after year thousands of people die regretting not having tried to accomplish all that they dreamed of doing. People who, like William Wallace said, are willing to exchange all the days of their life if they could only go back and change the path they decided to take.

I believe we develop a deep connection to stories like *Titanic*, *Braveheart*, and others like them because inside of us is a deep desire to live out similar stories, stories with a purpose.

Society, the expectations of others, and the ins-and-outs of the everyday have tamed us from considering the possibility of living out such lives. These things have redefined what it means to live a great story and they have sold us a completely different narrative as if it were truth. We have been trained to live a normal life, an ordinary life.

So here we are living in a largely unhappy society where thousands of people hate their jobs, are suffering from depression, boredom, and are living lives without purpose.

Let me be honest, a life with purpose is not as beneficial in the short run for the world economy as is the narrative that convinces you that a better television, the latest tablet, or a new car is what you need to be happy. Or, that the newest facial cream, work-out machine, or diet plan is what you need to be more beautiful. In the words of Steven Pressfield, "We live in a consumer culture that's acutely aware of its unhappiness and has massed all its profit-seeking artillery to exploit it. By selling us a product, a drug, a distraction."[2]

One of my wife's favorite movies is *Legends of the Fall*. She says she loves the plot of the film, but I think it's because it stars Brad Pitt.

It's a story of two brothers and the different path each decides to take in life. The narrative unfolds on lands owned by their father in the beautiful state of Montana. Alfred, the older brother leaves the lands he grew up on and moves to the city where he becomes a powerful business man and politician. Alfred achieves great success but in time loses his heart.

Then there's Tristan, the middle brother, played by Brad Pitt. John Eldredge writes about him in his book *Wild At Heart*. He says, "It is Tristan who embodies the West—he catches and rides the wild stallion, fights the grizzly with a knife, and wins the beautiful woman. I have yet to meet a man who wants to be Alfred or Samuel. I have yet to meet a woman who wants to marry one."[3]

I want to clarify something. I am not saying that anyone who wants to be successful, live in a city, or be a politician is living an empty life. Neither am I saying that we need to move out West, live in a tent, and fight with wild bears to live a life worth living.

The key to the story of *Legends of the Fall* lies in the fact that Alfred lost himself by falling in love with success, money, luxuries, and things, while Tristan decides to live his life aligned with his passion and calling.

The moment we begin watching this film, for a reason we will take up later in this book, our hearts connect with Tristan, not Alfred. In spite of this, many times we strive to become Alfreds instead of Tristans. We prefer to dedicate our whole lives to taking the safe route, and we forget how exciting and full a life of going after your dreams can be.

As a kid I was taught to play it safe. I'm not sure if that was due to the system I grew up in, or if it's simply because I was the first-born in a divorced home. But something made me cautious, practical, and pragmatic. My childhood didn't invite me to adventure, risk, or victory.

In spite of that, I remember being an inveterate superhero. For years I would dress as Superman or a Ghostbuster. My parents' friends would say I was "Superman of the Third World" because I would continue to wear my Superman costume months after Carnival had ended, complete with holes in the elbows and at the knees.

Like every kid, I had within me that innate drive for adventure, risk, and victory—a desire to be part of a larger cause, something that would benefit humanity.

> Always choosing what's safe kills the soul because risk and adventure are its oxygen.
> #innerherobook.com

But in time, that desire became dormant. Without realizing it, I had switched to the safe and ordinary road. Get good grades, go to university, get a good job, and live a successful life.

The problem isn't choosing one path over another; I am not judging any one route in particular. The problem is not listening to your heart. That is what happened to me. The mistake is in choosing the conventional road because it is the most travelled path to security, or to meeting the expectations of others, or to gaining a measure of success in the eyes of others. Always choosing what's safe kills the soul because risk and adventure are its oxygen.

I did everything expected on the path to the ordinary. I graduated from one of the best universities in Venezuela, began to work in one of the largest companies in the world where in less than ten years I began managing one of their most successful lines with sales that generated over a billion dollars. I married a spectacularly beautiful woman and had my first son, Benjamin, whom I love more than my own life.

Vacations and trips, a house in a beautiful neighborhood, cars, nice restaurants—despite all these amenities, and at the risk of sounding ungrateful, there was still an emptiness that unsettled my heart. It felt like I was living a boring life. It felt that there was a lot more of me that I could be giving.

What is troubling is that I am not alone in this. If I believed that this was a problem unique to only me, I would never have considered writing this book. But the sad truth is that I am not alone. Just by taking a look around me or talking with others, I could see people enslaved in their office cubicles, daydreaming of making a difference somewhere. Others were forced to work in poor-paying jobs because of being dealt a bad hand in life. Thousands of people cursing their Monday and dreaming every day of the coming Friday. Everyone silencing their songs, their desire to sing, paint, speak, or write, travel and see new places, transform, educate, or serve.

Is that what life is all about? About how quickly you can silence your song and kill your story? Are novels and movies made simply to give us a small window to temporarily satisfy our repressed desire to live full and meaningful lives? Is adventure, risk, and victory reserved only for fiction?

I don't believe so. That's why I wrote this book.

How am I so sure of that? Because I have begun to live it. The simple act of writing this book is one of my greatest adventures.

An adventure that fills me with fear, but at the same time makes me feel alive, like the time I spent a week in the mountains of Montana, or the first time I shot the rapids in a canoe. It makes me feel as alive as when I lie down with my son at night, and we look each other in the eyes for a few seconds without speaking until I see him drift off to sleep. He feels protected, and I feel like his protector.

Really, living a story that is worth living is not that difficult. It is simply an intentional process. If you don't decide to live your own story, you will end up living someone else's.

Within these pages, I am going to show you how to live out your own story. A story that, as my friend Todd Henry says, will cause you to "die empty" because you will have done everything that you came to this world to do.

> Really, living a story that is worth living is not that difficult. It is simply an intentional process. If you don't decide to live your own story, you will end up living someone else's. #innerherobook.com

THE HERO'S JOURNEY

THE HERO'S JOURNEY

THE NIGHT I MET DON, when I was confronted with the reality that I was living a boring life, my mind was racing a thousand miles an hour. I kept trying to figure out what my next step should be. Even though I realized that I was not living a fulfilling life, and there were stories that connected with the audience and stories that didn't, I wasn't sure how to build mine in a way that made it worth living. What's more, I wasn't sure what constituted a story and what didn't.

Right then and there, I made a commitment to learn everything I could about stories. I bought myself books by Donald Miller, Robert McKee, Christopher Vogler, and Joseph Campbell. I attended classes on how to create and tell them. I even asked Shane Meeker, historian for Procter & Gamble where I work, to teach me everything he knows about the power that stories hold.

Let me recount to you something that helped me understand the way great stories are told. When I was a boy, my grandmother gave me a piano. It was a beautiful piano that still graces the living room of my father's house. My grandmother wanted me to learn to play it, but for some reason that I do not recall well, I never did.

I remember being in music classes at a young age. I don't know if it was because I was bored, I wasn't any good, or if there was another reason, but at some point they took me out, and there were no more lessons for me.

For years the piano remained in my mother's house. It was simply a piece of living room decor. A decoration that was never used. I never had an interest in learning to play the piano, although sometimes I would open it and attempt a melody, one of those that only your mom would like, or perhaps because she was the only person who loved you enough to be willing to sit down and listen to you play.

I grew up and went to university. There I met my two best friends, Juan Carlos and Carlos. They're the kind of friends that life only gives you once; though you may meet new people whom you come to love very much, they will never be them.

Juan Carlos played piano. I discovered this one time when we were at his house studying for a university exam. But he didn't just play the piano, he was capable of bringing out the beauty of the music hidden inside the instrument; I would say he had a special gift. He practically taught himself how to play, and if you heard him play it would leave you breathless.

One day we were at a photography exhibit on campus when we suddenly caught a glimpse of a grand piano placed somewhat illogically in the middle of the exhibit hall. Wanting to experience the sound of a grand piano, Juan Carlos decided to play a song.

The moment he began to play, everyone in the room turned their attention from the exhibit to see where such a beautiful melody was coming from. Several drew near and leaned on the end of the piano so they could be nearer to the music and feel it more closely.

I perfectly recall two really cute girls walking up. And, I was single.

Though I struck my best Prince Charming pose, fixed my hair, and looked them in the eyes, they never took their eyes off Juan Carlos. They were smitten. If I didn't take over the piano at that very moment and break out an Alejandro Fernandez song, I wouldn't stand a chance.

I decided right then and there I was going to learn to play the piano. And that very day I began.

I remember my first class with Gerry Weil, one of the best jazz pianists in Latin America, who made me wait more than six months before he could fit me into his schedule so I could take lessons from him.

The first day, Gerry taught me the basics of music. He taught me that music is beautiful when it has form and follows a structure. Music, at its core, is quite mathematical and predictable. There are scales, rhythm, and harmonies that make it pleasing to our ears. Gerry would say, "In the end, it's all math. If you learn the formulas you will be fine. Learn the formulas and you'll know when to break them."

When I began to learn the them, I was amazed to see how many famous songs follow the same patterns and have the same chords and basic framework.

If I disregarded a structure, I only created noise; if I held to a structure, I created music. It was that simple. With time I learned that if you add certain dissonances within the framework, breaking the rules only slightly, you add flavor, making the music unique. But as a rule, if you don't want to simply generate noise, you had to follow its composition.

It's the same with stories. They have a predictable structure. If you don't follow it, you live a disorderly life, without meaning, or you're living a life that someone else wants you to live. If you learn story structure and follow it, you can create the narrative that you want, achieve your dreams, and get where you want to go.

Just like music, stories rely on structures, not on rules.

They rely on universal principles.

> It's the same with stories. They have a predictable structure.
> #innerherobook.com

The definition of a story in its most basic form is this: a a person, a hero, wants something and is willing to go through conflict to get it.

In other words, in order for us to create a story we need a person (whom we will call "the hero") who wants something (he needs to have defined goals and dreams) and is willing to go through conflict (he understands there is a price to pay and is willing to pay it) in order to obtain what he wants (the victory).

This person is you. You are the hero.

I believe, in general, we violate the three foundations of a story. First, we do not see ourselves as heroes. Second, we have not defined what it is we want from life. We think we have it defined, but the reality is that we don't. Third, we don't see conflict, struggle, or the antagonistic forces of our journey as necessary for the development of a story, but rather as life's hard knocks and bad luck.

I would like to clarify something. From now on I will use the term "hero" to identify the protagonist of the story—that is you. I will use the term to refer to both genders to avoid complicating the narrative of the book by using "hero" and "heroine" constantly.

> Regardless of
> whether you are
> a man or a woman,
> you are the hero
> of your story.
> #innerherobook.com

Regardless of whether you are a man or a woman, you are the hero of your story.

The search for the structure upon which great stories are based led me to become acquainted with the work of one of the men who revolutionized the art and science behind stories. Joseph Campbell was a mythologist, writer, and professor who at an early age became fascinated with the myths of different cultures and religions of the world. I don't know of anyone who has done a more thorough study on this topic.

Joseph Campbell discovered something very peculiar. He noted that the myths and stories of one culture closely resemble those of other cultures. It doesn't matter if they come from Asia or the American West, they are basically the same myths except they feature different characters.

This discovery led him to create the concept of the monomyth. In his own words, he describes it as follows:

Whether we listen with aloof amusement to the dreamlike mumbo jumbo of some red-eyed witch doctor of the Congo, or read with cultivated rapture thin translations from the sonnets of the mystic Lao-Tse, or now and again crack the hard nutshell of an argument of Aquinas, or catch suddenly the shining meaning of a bizarre Eskimo fairy tale, it will always be the one, shape-shifting yet marvelously constant story that we find, together with a challengingly persistent suggestion of more remaining to be experienced than will ever be known or told.[1]

This discovery by observation led him to develop one of the concepts, if not the concept, that has most influenced the process of the creation of stories known as "the hero's journey."

In it, Joseph Campbell put together a journey of clearly identified steps that guide the development of a hero's story. Departure from the ordinary world, what Campbell calls the "world of the everyday," heading toward an adventure, passing through trials and conflicts until achieving victory.

Years later, Christopher Vogler, then a Hollywood story analyst, wrote a seven-page document that revolutionized the Hollywood film industry. Vogler, profoundly impacted by the work of Joseph Campbell, wrote "A Practical Guide to *The Hero with a Thousand Faces*" with the initial objective of helping his colleagues at Walt Disney Studios to spot and write great stories.

It wasn't long before Vogler realized his work was having a real impact on Hollywood. He began to receive requests for his "Practical Guide" from different Hollywood studios. He was informed that different producers were handing out copies of his guide to writers, directors, and producers.

In his book *The Writer's Journey*, Vogler comments that his practical guide was required reading for any executive at Disney.[2] If you study the works of Joseph Campbell and Christopher Vogler you will realize that they have discovered and organized a template that defines the structure of the best Hollywood movies. *Star Wars*, *The Legend of Bagger Vance*, *Meet Joe Black*, *The Lord of the Rings*, *Legends of the Fall*, and thousands more have been powerfully influenced by the works of these two thinkers. The big question I asked myself was this: if Joseph Campbell and Christopher Vogler were capable of coming up with a structure that could create memorable stories, stories that connect with the human heart, could we apply the same structure to our own lives and create inspiring full lives of our own, ones that are truly worth living?

> The hero's journey will be a map and a structure that will guide you to live the life that you always dreamed of.
> #innerherobook.com

A resounding "yes" is the answer to this question, and it is the reason for the birth of this book. The hero's journey will be a map and a structure that will guide you to live the life that you always dreamed of. It will help you to understand where you are on your journey, and it will give you direction, like a compass, for the next step. It will protect you from falling into the almost invisible clutches of complacency, cynicism, and apathy. It will give you a hope like never before.

The hero's journey is a cycle of seven steps that begins and ends in the same place: the ordinary world. Let's take a look at the journey.

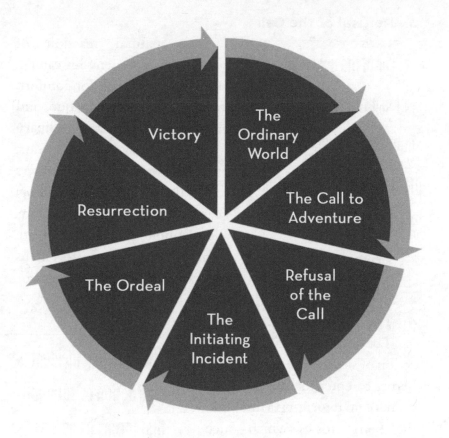

1. The Ordinary World

As Joseph Campbell explains, this is the world of the everyday. A world of the known, safe, and predictable. Independently of how we perceive it, whether it manifests itself as boredom or frustration in some, or as a mask of success for others, our hearts languish and we need risk and adventure. We are experiencing the death of the spirit.

2. The Call to Adventure

Something happens to destroy the idleness of our ordinary world. In the midst of the mere survival of our spirit, our heart finds strength where there is none and we remember our passion, our calling, and our plans for this world.

3. Refusal of the Call

Fear of the unknown, of failure, and of public humiliation create a force that tries to prevent us from setting out into adventure.
#innerherobook.com

The natural reaction of every hero is to deny his calling. Human beings look for comfort, maintaining the status quo, and playing it safe in the ordinary world. The easy road, our fears, or the expectations of others cause us to deny our calling. Fear of the unknown, of failure, and of public humiliation create a force that tries to prevent us from setting out into adventure.

4. The Initiating Incident

The initiating incident is the action or situation that forces us as heroes to enter the story. It is the point of no return; it is a threshold the hero crosses which once stepped over cannot be undone. We may either be forced into the story or we ourselves proactively seek to create circumstances that

The initiating incident is the action or situation that forces us as heroes to enter the story.
#innerherobook.com

immerse us into it. This is a key moment in our lives as heroes. From here we decide if we will flee back to the world of the ordinary or embark into the unknown of adventure.

5. The Ordeal

Conflict is indispensable in every great story.
#innerherobook.com

Conflict is indispensable in every great story. Struggles, obstacles, and trials are necessary as we evolve as a hero. Through them we learn to connect to the pain and suffering of others and make our lives an inspiring story. The story will be only as great, interesting, or inspiring as the level of conflict we are willing to overcome.

> The story will be only as great, interesting, or inspiring as the level of conflict we are willing to overcome. #innerherobook.com

6. Resurrection

We all reach the point where the opposing forces are so strong that we feel they have won. This is where the vast majority give up.

A hero is someone who is able to find strength inside of him when there is no strength left to draw from and is willing to rise up for one last battle. This is the point where you and I decide once and for all that we will not return to the ordinary world we left. At this point in the story, we have already won.

7. Victory

The basic structure of every story contains a hero who wants a treasure and must fight against adversity in order to obtain it. A story is not a story without a reward. A life without dreams, goals, or vision is a life not fully lived.

> A hero is someone who is able to find strength inside of him when there is no strength left to draw from and is willing to rise up for one last battle. #innerherobook.com

This is the moment when the hero gets his reward. He has overcome his obstacles, suffered, and won.

1. Return to the Ordinary World

Every hero deserves celebration, rest, and a time of restoration. This is why he returns to the ordinary world.

Nevertheless, this stage is risky because it can cause the hero to renew his love for the safety and security, the certainty of the ordinary world. After resurrection has occurred, a hero needs to undertake another adventure.

As you can see, the hero's journey is a never-ending cycle.

"So when does one retire?" I am sometimes asked.

"When you want to stop living and simply exist. Just look around you and observe what you see," I reply. "Don't ask, just observe. You'll see hundreds of people who died in their youths and are waiting around for someone to bury them when they get old."

"And when did they die?"

"When they fell in love with the ordinary world."

A story is not a story without a reward. A life without dreams, goals, or vision is a life not fully lived.
#innerherobook.com

CHAPTER 4

THE ORDINARY WORLD

EVERY GREAT STORY BEGINS in an ordinary world. Writers of great stories need a fixed point of reference from which the arc of the story will unfold to demonstrate the skill and bravery of the hero.

Every great story begins in an ordinary world. #innerherobook.com

Frodo in *The Lord of the Rings* lives happily in his shire. *The Hobbit* begins with Bilbo resting peacefully in front of his house. Clark Kent is living a quiet life as a member of a farming family long before he becomes Superman. Lucy in *The Chronicles of Narnia*, is playing hide-and-seek with her siblings before discovering the mystical closet that will lead them to the adventures waiting for them in the land of Narnia.

Joseph Campbell calls the ordinary world "the world of the everyday." This is the day-to-day world you and I inhabit. A world filled with routine and void of the new, of the unpredictable.

One of the clearest cases of the power of the ordinary world is seen in movie *The Shawshank Redemption*[1] in which Brooks, already an old man, has spent more than 50 years in prison, and is released on parole.

Unexpectedly, Brooks gets news of his freedom but then attempts to kill a cellmate. Fortunately, his friends are able to convince him not to go through with it.

Why does Brooks attempt to kill one of his cellmates after receiving the long-awaited news of his release?

Because of fear.

Brooks has spent over fifty years behind bars. Although he theoretically desires freedom, the moment he gets it he is overcome with fear. Prison has become his home. Within its walls, he is a somebody. Outside of them, he is a nobody. So great is his fear that he finds himself on the verge of murdering a fellow inmate in order to remain imprisoned, to continue to live in "his ordinary world."

Like Brooks, we also unconsciously fight to keep ourselves locked in the world of the familiar. We fear change because it makes us vulnerable. In the ordinary world we know how to win, things come easily for us, and they are predictable. The ordinary world feeds our egos. It makes us feel successful; it makes us feel invincible.

The lure of the ordinary world keeps people tied to jobs they hate. It keeps some women tied to violent relationships, societies tied to corrupt

> We fear change because it makes us vulnerable.
> #innerherobook.com

leaders, and it keeps individuals tied to routines that make their lives deeply boring.

My own natural tendency is to fall into the flow of safe routines and end up living a life of utter boredom.

The interesting thing about all of this is that we as creatures are given over to exploration. We learn by trial and error. From the time we are babies, little by little, we begin creating our own ordinary worlds.

From birth, life is about exploration. What's more, we have an innate passion for it. Even though some children are more cautious than others, all of us in some way or another gets bumps and bruises when we are learning to walk, we stick our finger in a light socket, or we jump from a height too great for us.

As we grow, we begin to learn and come to understand our environment in view of our successes and failures.

Over time, depending on how secure we are in ourselves, we begin to develop a fear of failure and an understanding of our limitations for success.

When we learn the limitations of our success we want to stay within those bounds. Likewise, we try to avoid situations where success is less certain. Over time, we begin to create invisible walls around us that keep us imprisoned and prevent us from getting out and exploring new horizons.

This is why, day after day, we follow the same routines, eat at the same places, order the same meals, with the same group of friends, and tell the same jokes over and over again. We live in a microcosm that we begin to believe is the world at large, but it is not. Some years ago I met a multimillionaire who had never left his hometown and had no intention of ever doing so. I met another man who only ever ate the same four foods. I once heard about a woman who went back to

> We live in a microcosm that we begin to believe is the world at large, but it is not.
> #innerherobook.com

the same abusive husband time and time again for the sole purpose of waiting for the next episode to grieve over.

> I want to convince you that even though keeping ourselves in the ordinary world helps us feel safe and secure, in time it kills the soul, because the soul needs adventure and risk.
> #innerherobook.com

> There are no great stories in the ordinary world; they simply does not exist.
> #innerherobook.com

This chapter is not meant to give you a solution to the problems of the ordinary world. That's what the next four chapters are for. The objective of this chapter is for you come to the conclusion that your ordinary world exists and that you may in some way be trapped in it. I want to convince you that even though keeping ourselves in the ordinary world helps us feel safe and secure, in time it kills the soul, because the soul needs adventure and risk. A soul feeds on those things.

Imagine if Frodo in *The Lord of the Rings* had stayed in the shire. What would the movie *Gladiator* be like if Maximus had returned home as he requests the king to let him do and lived the rest of his life with his wife and kids? And what if Luke Skywalker had stayed with his uncle, denying his calling to become a Jedi? All of the great stories that we see in movie theaters or read about in a good book have a hero who decides to leave or is expelled from his ordinary world. There are no great stories in the ordinary world; they simply does not exist. We did not come to this world to live in the world of the ordinary.

My desire for you is that you don't come to the end of your life having lived most of it in the ordinary world. If you are coming to realize that you have been a prisoner of the ordinary world, you need to begin to get out of it. The following chapters will help you in the process.

CHAPTER 5

THE CALL TO ADVENTURE

SCOTT HARRISON WAS BORN IN PHILADELPHIA and raised in a Christian home. He formed a band in high school and later moved to New York to try his hand at making it a success, hoping to live the life he'd always dreamed of.

In New York though his band had begun to have a certain amount of success, they didn't give themselves sufficient time to achieve the contract they dreamed of. Speaking candidly, Scott admitted everyone hated each other, and, eventually, the band broke up.

When it happened, Scott was immersed in the bar scene which included parties and alcohol. With no band, he tried to consider what his next step should be. Scott realized that the guy that was promoting his band was making good money, so he decided to partner with him and began a new career as a promoter in New York City.

Little by little, he began to be successful. The time came when he was so successful that liquor companies would pay him thousands of dollars to drink their brand. He was so well known in that world that he was trained to move his wrist quickly so that in photos they took of him, his gold Rolex watch appears at just the perfect angle. At just twenty-eight years old he not only had a Rolex, but a grand piano, a BMW, and a girlfriend who was a model for billboards and magazines.

Scott admits that he took massive amounts of drugs, not because he was addicted, but because life seemed utterly boring. Despite an abundance of "things" his life lacked any real meaning. One New Year's, Scott traveled with some friends to Punta del Este to enjoy a spectacular vacation. Everything had been planned to perfection: nights of poker, fireworks, horses, dinners, servants, etc.

But, the trip changed Scott forever. While he was there, he received a call to adventure. Through the process of deep reflection, Scott came to realize that he was one of the worst people he knew. Success had made him arrogant and egotistical. He could clearly see in himself and in those around him the consequences their line of work produced. Scott finally admitted that he was emotionally, spiritually, and morally bankrupt.[1]

When Scott got back to New York a small change had taken place inside of him. There was a calling in his heart to do something different. He said, "What if I decided to serve God? But not in the hypocritical manner I saw as a kid, but instead, what if I actually served others?[2]

Scott decided to give a year of his life to a humanitarian cause. He left everything he had behind and began the search for his adventure.

As in Scott's case, normally the call to adventure doesn't come clearly defined, but it's something that we feel within. It is something enormous that calls us—as if we were born for it. For some, the call is something gigantic that will change their lives forever. For others, there will be small steps that will cause you to tell a story that you never imagined. No matter how it happens, we can begin to catch on to what it is if we reflect on what we are passionate about.

> The call to adventure doesn't come clearly defined, but it's something that we feel within.
> #innerherobook.com

Passion

How can we discover our passion? This is a question I asked myself for years and one which I am constantly asked by followers of my blog and podcast.

A clear connection exits between calling and passion. Passion is like a little clue, that small flashlight that illuminates the next few feet in front of us when we enter the fog of a dark night. If we want to discover our calling, we need to follow our passion.

One of the greatest problems I have seen is that people don't clearly understand what the word *passion* means. Many people define it as an inclination, preference, or strong desire towards a person or a thing. And we do understand passion in that way.

I have a passion for the mountains and being in direct contact with nature and my Creator. I get excited about a particular ball game, or I love to eat barbecued pork ribs every chance I get. Some are passionate about running while others are deeply satisfied playing with their dog. Some people have a passion for bringing justice to the needy while others are passionate about maintaining their profiles on social networks.

If passion is simply an inclination, preference, or strong desire how do we differentiate between the passion that connects us to our calling and passion for eating barbecued pork ribs, or for exercising, or for watching our favorite program? The concept of passion, the one that I want to define in this book, is something bigger, broader, and more inspiring.

Remember my friend Dave, the one who took me to meet Donald Miller? He constantly goes around thinking up great ideas. One night when we were having dinner together we decided to discuss the concept of passion.

"What is passion for you, Dave?" I asked him.

After he gave me a predictable answer in which he explained to me, in clichés, that passion is that which brings him life, emotion, etc., he paused for a second and said:

"My passion comes not only from what I like to do, my passion also comes from what I hate the most."

Now we were onto something interesting, something worthy of putting in a book.

"You know," he said, "I hate and am angered over many things. Some of those things are insignificant, they're just not important. Like when I get stuck in traffic or my cell phone battery dies. But there are other things, hmm…, there are others," I could see the fire in his eyes, as if he were about to eliminate me like in an X-Men movie, "that I can't tolerate! I can't stand them so much that I have to do something about changing them. Extreme poverty, sexual slavery, a lack of basic necessities such as food, water, and education in third-world countries. Those things that make my blood boil."

> "My passion comes not only from what I like to do, my passion also comes from what I hate the most."
> #innerherobook.com

Thanks to that passion, Dave decided to use his coffee distribution company not only to sell excellent coffee and make a profit, but also to educate communities in Central America in the proper coffee production so they can become self-sustaining, develop as a community, and escape poverty.

So, passion deals with desires or inclinations towards the good, but it also takes into account what you despise or cannot stand. But there was still something missing. Why is it that so many of us have desires or inclinations toward one thing, or, like Dave, a rage or rejection for another, but still we do nothing about it, nor do we make any difference?

I believe there has to be something about the nature of passion that requires you to be moved to make a difference. If something doesn't move you, it isn't passion.

Which brings me to another friend, Todd Henry.

I met Todd through one of those miracles of destiny. A friend of a friend of the brother of a friend heard that I was about to write a book and introduced me to him.

Todd was the creative director of the biggest church in Cincinnati where weekly attendance runs between fifteen and twenty thousand people. Todd, as a creative, is a deep thinker. As a result of a fervent desire to educate others and celebrate the creative process of the human being, he started a podcast that exploded in popularity and later led him to become a full-time writer and speaker.

Todd is an expert in the area of passion. As a matter of fact, his book *Die Empty: Unleash Your Best Work Every Day,* dedicates an entire chapter to what he calls productive passion.

Productive passion is that kind of passion that inevitably leads you to take action. In talking with him he said to me, "Passion isn't just excitement and enthusiasm. Passion has another side to it, one of suffering." Simply look up the definition of the word *passion* in the dictionary and you will find two definitions that appear to be diametrically opposed to one

> "Passion is something you are willing to suffer for in order to achieve it."
> #innerherobook.com

other: "desire and inclination" on the one hand and "affliction and suffering" on the other.

In Todd's words: "Passion is something you are willing to suffer for in order to achieve it."

Now we've arrived at the correct definition of passion. Passion comes from a strong desire or inclination; it also can come from anger or rejection of something unjust or incorrect in this world; but, in the end, it's something we need to be willing to suffer for.

> it's something we need to be willing to suffer for.
> #innerherobook.com

You need to define your passion.

There are certain questions that can help you in the process. What are some of the things you have a strong preference or deep desire toward? What do you feel is more a calling than a job? Have you ever felt like you were born for something? Is there something that makes you angry, or that you strongly disapprove of?

After you have answered some or all of these questions, verify your answers asking yourself the following:

When I am doing what I defined as passion, am I still enthusiastic and thinking about what I need to do tomorrow? Does my passion motivate my imagination? If I were to inherit a million dollars, would I continue to what I have defined as my passion?

Defining your passion is a critical step. In general, people avoid doing it because they think they already know what it is that they want. The reality is that it's a process of much introspection and it's not simple. Remember, your passion is like a flashlight that lights your way through the fog on a dark night. If you don't have your passion defined, you will start your adventure without a flashlight and you may end up frustrated and in a place you never intended.

> Remember, your passion is like a flashlight that lights your way through the fog on a dark night.
> #innerherobook.com

Defining your passion is not the only step. Many cheap motivational speakers convince you that passion is the only thing needed to achieve your dreams. "Simply do what you have a passion for and you will be happy," is common rhetoric.

That may be true if you have a millionaire dad who maintains you. But it's not reality for most. Defining your passion is crucial and the most important step, but it's not the only one. You need to understand that your efforts have to be guided by the intersection of your passion, your skills, and the market.

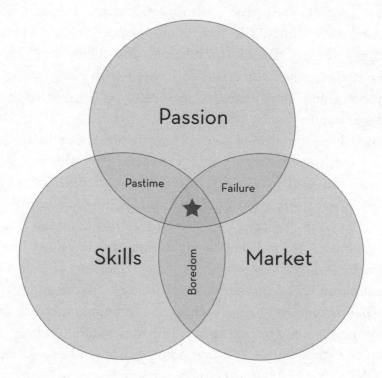

Skills

After the disheartening experience of the two cute girls swooning over my friend Juan Carlos upon hearing him play the piano which led me to take up the instrument so I wouldn't end up single the rest of my life, I became passionate about music. It was no longer for the girls, but rather for the pleasure of creating something that didn't exist before, following the structures, scales, and melodies of the art of music.

Over time, I got better and better but never to the point of being a professional pianist. The time eventually came when I had to decide if it would become my future or just a delightful hobby, restorative and necessary, but, in the end, just a hobby.

One of the most common errors that I encounter is that people think that if they are passionate about something, then they're automatically good at it. They think that the simple fact that they have passion gives them a competitive edge in that area.

The truth is that it gives you a competitive edge when you compare yourself with people who haven't worked in that field or developed that ability, like the piano giving me a competitive advantage over my friends and relatives. But, when you enter the world of music, when you compare yourself with pianists who have been playing since they were five years old, you realize that they are in another league.

Now, there are things you are passionate about that you are good at. It is important that discover them. But, this is a process in which you will need to be brutally honest with yourself. In order to answer this question, you can look to your family, your friends, or your mentor. You need to reflect and ask yourself, *What are my strengths? What are my weaknesses? What am I better at than others?*

I am reminded of another one of my closest friends and mentors, Peter Blanco. The guy is a machine. I remember training on my bike for months only to ride against him and watch him beat me on a cheap and rusty bicycle. At one point, I decided I would jog one hour a day for several months only to see him leave me behind in the dust without mercy in mere seconds.

Peter did karate and he would always tell me when someone hit him, it never hurt. For whatever reason, maybe because he trained so much as a kid or maybe it was just his genetic makeup, but punches never hurt him. I'm not kidding, sometimes several of us would compete to see who could hit him on the shoulder with all of our strength only to have him laugh and make us turn and run when he decided to break us in two.

These are the types of abilities that I am referring to. If you will reflect upon it, I'm sure you'll recognize certain strengths you have inside of you. In the same way that any physical activity or sport are a cinch for Peter, for you it might be you have the ability to negotiate or the ability to empathize with others, or serve others without expecting anything in return. Maybe you are funny and upbeat, maybe when you put together an outfit, everybody comments on it. You have amazing strengths. You just need to get quiet and listen to yourself.

> You have amazing strengths. You just need to get quiet and listen to yourself. #innerherobook.com

Many years ago, I undertook one of my greatest risks. I decided to open a multi-service telecommunications store. It was a huge investment, so I had to find a very special person who believed in me.

With money in hand, I rented a place and began to remodel it. I quickly paid for the telecommunications equipment and began to plan the installation so I'd be ready upon its arrival. With more than 80% of the money already invested and with no chance of getting it back, the board of directors of the building where my business would be located unanimously decided I could not install the antennae necessary for the day-to-day operation of the business. After a slew of meetings, doors slammed in my face, and letters sent back and forth on the issue, they decided to put it to a vote in an official meeting with the entire building. When I got to the meeting, I was deeply distraught. The voting was beginning, and I was hit with the fact that I was going to lose by a unanimous vote with hardly any type of negotiation having taken place. In my desperation, I decided to speak up. I don't remember exactly what I said but I do remember, little by little, as I was speaking people began to empathize with my situation. I could see how, almost miraculously, many of them changed their stance. I don't know if it was out of compassion or conviction, but they decided to vote on my behalf. That night, I won the vote in a way I would not have imagined.

But, the most important thing from that evening was not that I got the vote. The most important thing was that I did not fully understand what had happened. I began to realize that I possessed a strength in the arena of communicating. I felt that in some way, if I believed in what I was speaking about, I could bring people around to a new way of thinking. This was the seed that later grew into many things, including my blog, a podcast, and this book.

Remember to dedicate some time to reflecting on this. The answer is not just in defining your passions. You need to determine your strengths. You need to discover your competitive edge.

Marketability

Why do we need to talk about marketability? Because if you only have passion and skills but no market, all you have is a hobby.

Most people want to be able to live off of their passion. Can you imagine living day to day earning money doing what you are passionate about? What would your life be like if your passion became a reality?

> The answer is not just in defining your passions. You need to determine your strengths. You need to discover your competitive edge.
> #innerherobook.com

This is a question that you need to answer for yourself. There is nothing wrong with having a hobby. But if you want to live off of your passion, you need to be sure that there is a need for it in the marketplace.

Now I am not necessarily saying that you need to capitalize on your passion. You may want to use it as a volunteer. But in the end, there has to be a need in the market that you will meet with your service, your art, your consulting, your time, etc.

That is why companies invest millions of dollars in market research. They need to be sure that a market exists that will resonate with the product or service that they are designing.

These companies have sometimes realized that in being so far removed from the consumer, an idea that inspires the leader of a company may be totally useless in the eyes of the costumer. Several years ago I had the opportunity to personally meet Gary Vaynerchuk, a celebrity who became a multimillionaire using the Internet, and learned first-hand the story of how he achieved success.

Gary was born in the former Soviet Union, but he grew up in New Jersey. From a young age, he had the opportunity to work helping out at his dad's liquor store. During those years he discovered something very interesting. Gary discovered that customers who came to buy wine he acted completely different from the clients that came to buy other types of liquor.

For example, if someone came to buy whiskey, it didn't matter what Gary or his dad recommended, they purchased the brand they had decided on beforehand. On the other hand, when a customer came in to buy wines, he would act totally different. This type of customer was an explorer. He would ask questions and was open to trying new labels and vintages. Very early on, Gary realized that there was a gap in the market for those seeking to be educated about wine.

With wine as his passion coupled with the experience gained from working in his father's store, he knew he was a good at guiding and educating consumers to try different types of wine. In 2006, he launched *Wine Library TV*, a show on YouTube that become a major platform for wine education and distribution. Gary catapulted sales at his dad's liquor store from four million dollars a year to more than sixty million dollars a year with over half of his sales made online.

Gary discovered a need in the market and committed himself to educate wine-lovers using simple and light-hearted messages. The rest is history.

Many times people ask me how they can determine if there is a market. The answer is simple. First, think about service. If you have a passion for something and you are good at it, then begin to think about how you can serve those around you. Do you like baking and are you good at it? Bake and give your goods to someone in need and observe their reaction. Do you like to teach children? Start doing it for free in order to gain experience and to find out whether there is a need for your service.

That is how my blog started, which at the time of writing these lines is visited by more than one million people a year. I discovered that my passion was leadership, helping others discover their purpose, and motivating them to take their journey. I also felt I had a strength in communicating. Thus, I launched liderazgohoy.com.

For several years up to the present, I have written and published podcasts and videos completely free of charge. I needed to know if there was a market for my message. I needed to confirm that my passion would resonate with an audience.

Today I have book contracts and I am paid good money as a speaker. But, everything began as a service to others. That is how I discovered my voice. That is how I discovered my market. That is how I discovered my niche.

Another one of the more common errors I observe is people aligning their life plan with only two of the three aspects—passion, skill, and marketability—that we have discussed. Keep in mind the following:

- If you have a passion for something and you are good at it, but there is no market with it, then what you have is a hobby. There is nothing wrong in having a hobby, but it is important that you be honest and define it as such.
- If you have a passion for something and there is a market for it, but you are not good at it, you are walking straight into frustration, failure, and mediocrity. You will never reach the level of those who have an innate ability for it, and you will live a life full of frustration. (I wish to be clear in this point that when I refer to "not being good" at something, I am not referring to an ability that you can develop with effort and persistence, but rather to an

ability that is impossible for you to reach at a professional level. For example, if I wanted to become an Olympic ice-skater at my age and with no prior experience.

- If you are good at something and there is a market, but you don't have a passion for it, you will live a profoundly boring life. This group is the one that I normally refer to when I say that "they curse their Monday and they spend every day waiting for Friday." They are good at what they do, maybe they even get paid well for doing it, but they have no passion for their occupation.

In summary, the takeaway is this: in order to find your calling, you need to identify the area where your passion, skills, and the market meet. That is the secret.

Sources That Will Nurture Your Passion

Curtis Martin was born in 1973 surrounded by violence, alcohol and drugs. His mother had to raise him alone after his father abandoned them to go after a life of alcohol and drugs. The violence that Curtis grew up in was so bad that his grandmother was found dead, stabbed to death. He too came close to death when a loaded gun pointed at his head misfired seven times.

Martin was considered a great athlete as a kid and quickly became a star football player in high school. In time, he not only made it to the NFL but became one of the best players in the league. And, in 2012, he received the MVP award for being the most valuable player of the year.

In his award speech, he left everyone speechless when he admitted to having never liked American football.

> In order to find your calling, you need to identify the area where your passion, skills, and the market meet. That is the secret.
> #innerherobook.com

Let me put this in perspective. Americans are fanatical about football. Hundreds of thousands of kids play this sport from a young age with the dream of someday going pro.

Only a limited percentage of children can play on a high school football team. Of those, a small percentage gets to play in college. And of these, an even smaller percentage reaches the professional level.

And of those that reach the professional level, only one is named MVP of the year. In other words, just one of a limited percentage, of another small percentage, of an even smaller percentage gets the prize. And, he didn't even care for the sport!

After Curtis Martin admitted his lack of passion for the game, he commented that the reason he decided to play was because he was convinced that the platform that football would create for him could be used to do good for humanity.

His passion wasn't in football. His passion was using the sport—including the fame and money it had brought him—to invest in causes that were near and dear to his heart.

In his award speech he said, "I knew that if I was going to be successful at playing football, I would need a cause to play for greater than the sport itself because love for the game was not in my heart."[3]

Not everyone has a passion for that they do. However, that does not mean they don't have a passion for the results or why they do it. Many times we think we don't have a passion for something simply because we're only looking at passion as coming from one specific source.

There are three sources that will nurture your passion: passion for the activity itself and what you do, passion for the results of what you do, and passion for whom you do it.

1. Passion For What You Do. This is the most common source of passion. Do you like doing what you do? If you were to inherit a million dollars, would you still continue doing this activity? If your answers are affirmative, it is probable that this is the source that nurtures your passion.

I will never forget my friend Daniel from university. Daniel left a lucrative career at Procter & Gamble to pursue his passion—teaching others how to dance. I remember he lived dancing, breathed dancing, ate dancing. Dancing was his world, his dream, and his passion.

All of us wish we could dedicate our day-to-day activity to doing what we are passionate about. But there are other sources of passion. Sometimes our work itself doesn't ignite our passion, but rather the results that we obtain from that work.

2. **Passion For The Results.** Last year I had the opportunity to have lunch with the owner of one of the largest multilevel companies in the world. During our conversation, we touched on the topic of passion, and he said something that surprised me: "I have never liked the multilevel business," he said. "I hate cold calls, the talks, the sales, and the rejection. I've never liked it that people who earn thirty times less than I do stand in front of me and tell me that my business isn't working. I hate every bit of it

"Then why did you do it?" I asked him.

"For the payoff. Just for the payoff. Nothing else would give me the freedom to be with my family and allow me to do what I wanted to do. I didn't want to be employed, even if it offered good pay. I wanted to travel, to eat lunch with my kids. My passion is my family, and that is why I do it."

This story is quite common. I'm constantly talking to athletes who despise the intense training they have to go through or business men and women who have no passion in their day-to-day work routines. But, they are deeply passionate about the payoff of what they do.

In the end, it is a personal decision. There are people who are passionate about what they do and also about the profits. But, if that is not the case, what is your priority? Passion for what you do? Then make sure you love what you do, day in, day out. Then decide on the sacrifices you will make in order to obtain the outcome you desire.

But there is another source of passion that, as in the case of Curtis Martin, is the most powerful of the three: passion for whom you do it.

3. Passion For Who You Do It For. Just like Curtis said in his award speech for MVP of the year, he played football in order to develop a platform that allowed him to do good to others. He had to "play for a greater cause because there was no love for football in his heart."

This is one of the most powerful sources of passion that exists, and it's one of the most overlooked. In this case it may be that you are not passionate about what you do, and you are not passionate about the results that you will get personally, but you are passionate about the results that it will bring for someone you love deeply, or the positive change that you will bring about in the life of another person.

One great example of this source of passion is the thousands of people that have dedicated their lives to fighting for social justice in one form or another. Many of them don't like the sacrifices, the low salaries, or in many cases, the precarious conditions of the countries where they have to travel and work. But to see social justice made real on the earth is what makes them passionate like nothing else.

By the way, remember Scott Harrison, whom I wrote about at the beginning of the chapter? After asking himself the question about serving God and others, he embarked on an adventure that eventually led him to found charity: water.

From 2006 to 2014, charity: water, a nonprofit corporation that invests one hundred percent of its donations to bring water to the needy, has managed to bring clean water to 4.1 million human beings who had no clean water to drink.

> Neither God nor life will leave you in the ordinary world without calling you on an adventure. You were not born for the ordinary world.
>
> #innerherobook.com

The clean water that more than four million people receive daily thanks to Scott following his calling, is much more than just water. Water is life. Clean water means fewer illnesses, which means children can go to school, which also means they can study and graduate, which means that clean water is pulling the world out of poverty.

Neither God nor life will leave you in the ordinary world without calling you on an adventure. You were not born for the ordinary world. You were born for something more. There is another road you can take, a different bridge you must dare to cross. Another kind of treasure worth fighting for.

In the words of my friend Marco Ayuso, "To discover your passion is to turn on your light. Doing what you're passionate lights up the world."[4]

> To discover your passion is to turn on your light. Doing what you're passionate about lights up to the world. #innerherobook.com

CHAPTER 6

THE TREASURE

THE BASIC CONCEPT OF A STORY is a hero wants something and is willing to go through an ordeal to get it. That something the hero wants must be substantial enough to make his ordeal worthwhile. That something is the treasure.

In every film, the hero has a clear reason to embark upon an adventure. Rudy Ruettiger, who inspired the film *Rudy*, was sure of his dream to play football for the University of Notre Dame team when he decided to quit his job to try and gain admission to the prestigious university. Maximus in *Gladiator* wants justice for the murder of his family and Emperor Marcus Aurelius. Frodo in *Lord of the Rings* wants to destroy the ring, and William Wallace in *Braveheart* wants to free Scotland. In a fight, the treasure needs to be clearly defined in the moment that the call to adventure occurs. If the audience doesn't have a clear reason why the

> Nobody gets close, not even remotely, to the risk involved in an adventure, without a clear idea of the possible prize.
> #innerherobook.com

hero decides to fight, they automatically lose interest. No hero embarks upon an adventure without a clear treasure. Nobody gets close, not even remotely, to the risk involved in an adventure, without a clear idea of the possible prize.

What is unfortunate is that oftentimes we go through life without the necessary vision of where it is exactly we want to get. We invest years planning a wedding, weeks planning a vacation, days planning a birthday party, but oftentimes we won't give a few hours deciding what we want out of life.

However, investing a little bit of time defining it will make all the difference. John Goddard did so when he was only fifteen. I read his story some years ago in the book *Chicken Soup for the Soul* by Jack Canfield and Mark Victor Hansen. John Goddard managed to define what he wanted in life.

> Spending a little bit of time defining what you want out of life will make all the difference.
> #innerherobook.com

John put up a list of a 127 dreams to fulfill and called it My Life List. He didn't write trivial goals on his list, but rather, large-scale dreams, such as climbing some of the highest mountains in the world, visiting the North and South Poles, seeing the Eiffel Tower, writing a book, building a telescope, crossing the Grand Canyon, reading the Bible all the way through, running a mile in less than five minutes, taking off and landing on an aircraft carrier, learning Spanish, French, and Arabic, getting married, and having a family.[1]

This list delineated John's future because it helped him direct each step of his way. About this, John remarked:

Since my early childhood, I always dreamed of becoming an explorer.... Somehow, I had the impression that an explorer was someone who lived in the jungle with natives and many wild animals and I couldn't ever imagine anything better than that! Unlike other children who changed their minds several times as they were growing up about what they wanted to be in their lives, I never had any doubts about my ambition.[2]

John passed away on May 17, 2013. He lost his battle against a rare type of cancer. He was eighty-eight years old. Famous newspapers wrote about the death of "the real Indiana Jones." John had lived a life worth telling.

John had not only achieved all the dreams I mentioned previously, but he had become the first explorer to travel the Nile River from end to end by kayak, he climbed the Kilimanjaro, he broke the record speed of an F-111 aircraft by taking it to more than 1,500 miles per hour. He had climbed twelve of the highest mountains in the world and visited practically all the countries in the world. He wrote two books, *The Survivor* and *Kayaks Down the Nile*. He had six children, ten grandchildren, and two great-grandchildren.

Of the 127 goals that John set for himself when he was fifteen, he achieved 109. One or two of them would have meant the experience of a lifetime for many of us, but John had accomplished 109 of them.

John was once asked about his list, and his answer was, "Most people say 'someday'…and that means nothing. It is important to write it down and place it where you can see it every day."[3]

I imagine that if I had had the opportunity to meet John, it would have been magical, as his friends say. I am sure that John would have had more than one story to tell. It would have been like meeting one of the best explorers in the world, a musician, a photographer, and a writer all at the same time. A great husband and inspiring family man.

The big difference between John and any other person with similar dreams is that John wrote

> There is an almost magical power in the act of writing down your dreams and goals.
> #innerherobook.com

them down on a piece of paper. John was intentional about what he wanted to accomplish and made it happen.

There is an almost magical power in the act of writing down your dreams and goals. An effort that has already been confirmed by many people.

Goals have to be specific and contain a date. Failing to put a date on your goals will transform your dreams into the "someday" that John Goddard referred to.

Writing down your dreams and goals will transform your life and give you the necessary guidance to write the story that you wish to live and tell. Here are some of the positive aspects of writing them down:

1. It forces you to clarify what you want. When I started my marketing career at Procter & Gamble, I discovered one of most difficult areas to develop and one that is part of the culture of this organization is writing.

At Procter & Gamble every idea, project, or requisition is handled with the famous one-pager. From your everyday work plans to complex global projects, everything is presented to management in a one-page document.

> Writing down your dreams and goals will transform your life and give you the necessary guidance to write the story that you wish to live and tell.
> #innerherobook.com

The culture of writing at Procter & Gamble is one of the most powerful competitive advantages of the organization. After a couple of years, any manager has written hundreds of these kind of documents. Courses lasting several days are provided in which you are taught how to write.

The reason the company puts so much emphasis on the one-pager is that it forces you to organize and define your ideas. There is no way to write down a bad idea that can make it sound like a good one. The company management has understood that the writing process helps managers learn to think correctly, organize their ideas, tell a story that has meaning, and ultimately influences the organization. Writing also helps the organization document everything that has been agreed on so they can go back in case of doubts or misunderstandings.

If the power of writing is considered a cornerstone in a large corporation like Procter & Gamble, you should also consider it a cornerstone in developing your life. The same benefits obtained by the company are available to you.

Writing down your goals requires you to think, to organize, and to prioritize what you want from life. Writing down your goals helps you distinguish what's trivial from what's important, what's urgent from what can wait. Another incredibly beneficial aspect is that writing down your goals helps you keep them in mind, to change directions if necessary, and to eliminate the ones that are no longer relevant to your life.

2. It helps you maintain focus and filter your opportunities. Writing down your dreams and goals gives you focus. How do you think John Goddard would have responded if in his twenties or thirties he had gotten a very attractive corporate job offer with high growth potential both in salary and as a professional? I am sure he would have declined it. Why? Because none of his 127 goals was to become director, vice-president, or CEO of a corporation. What's more, even if that opportunity had been good for John in many respects, it would have kept him away from his real dreams.

We see another amazing story of focus in the largest coffee shop chain, Starbucks.

Starbucks was founded in 1971 and grew rapidly in the United

> Writing down your goals requires you to think, to organize, and to prioritize what you want from life.
> #innerherobook.com

States and later worldwide. It now has more than 23,000 stores around the world.

However, Starbucks's expansion was not always easy. Between 2005 and 2008 sales in the stores went down because the rapid growth of the organization made them lose their focus. The stores weren't just selling coffee but a huge variety of opportunities that had them distracted—the addition of breakfast, CD sales, coffee makers, etc.

In January 2008, the board of directors decided to bring back Howard Schultz, one of their most brilliant CEOs, with the main purpose of recovering the level of growth that the company once had.

One of the first decisions made by Schultz—necessary, but extremely difficult—was to close down all the stores in the US for one day to retrain the staff on how to serve the best possible cup of coffee. That decision to close all the stores for one day cost Starbucks seven million dollars.

The work Schultz accomplished was refocus the organization, teaching them that before they sold breakfasts, CDs, or coffee makers, they needed to be the very best at making coffee. About this, Schultz remarked:

> We began to make a permanent promise to ourselves and our customers: The proof of everything we do has to be in the cup of coffee….
>
> I believe that what I was trying to do was to let everybody know that it was not about Howard Schultz, it was not about thousands of coffee shops, it was about one coffee shop, it was about an extraordinary cup of coffee and a commitment...to do everything possible to exceed our customers's expectations.[4]

The story of Starbucks is a story of focus and how a company that lost its focus almost destroyed itself. Nevertheless, it is also a story of redemption and how, by going back to focusing the team, you can once again move forward.

As you become more successful, you will notice that more and more opportunities will start coming to you. Some of them will accelerate the achievement of your dreams and goals, but others will pull you away from them. That is why, in the same way that Starbucks decided to cancel the launch of their hot breakfasts and many other things in order to focus on coffee, and in the same way that John Goddard laughed at a corporate job offer, writing down your dreams and goals will help you to stay on course and ensure that you get back home. Writing down your goals and dreams will help you to be able to say *no* to many things so you can say *yes* to others.

> Writing down your goals and dreams will help you to be able to say *no* to many things so you can say *yes* to others.
> #innerherobook.com

3. It helps you to focus on achievement, not on the process. The process—from the time you set your goal until you achieve it—is difficult. Later on, we will go into everything that constitutes the ordeal, its obstacles, hard knocks, and failures. But the point here is that the ordeal is a painful and difficult process, and it's full of suffering. If your dream is big enough, you will have to pass through it.

Writing down your goals will help you in the midst of the conflict, to focus on the reward. This will give you enough energy to keep plugging away, day after day, toward your life dreams. While some people give up because they are focused on the ordeal and its suffering, hard knocks, and failures, others make their dreams come true by focusing on the reward.

After making up your mind to start exercising or eating healthy to benefit your health, have you ever given up? I have. I can assure you if your answer is also affirmative the reason you quit exercising or dieting is that you focused on the process and lost your focus on the goal.

Focusing on the process causes all your energy to dissipate, by bemoaning that you have to get up early to go for a run, or that you have to stop at the gym after work when you are already tired, or that you can't eat this or that. This is focusing on the process.

On the other hand, focusing on the goal is keeping in mind the person that you will become, the medal that will be placed around your neck, your weight on the scales, or the excellent results you will get on your medical exam. Where you choose to focus will make an enormous difference, and writing down your dreams and goals will help you focus on the right thing

I remember the time I decided to climb El Pico Bolivar in Merida, Venezuela. It's the highest peak in the Venezuelan Andes, a majestic mountain of 16,332 feet where a bust of the great liberator, Simon Bolivar, is located.

Years before my adventure, my mother had given me a picture of my uncle, her brother, next to the bust of Bolivar there at the top of the mountain.

That same feat had become my goal too. My dream was to put both pictures side by side. One of my uncle, who is fifty years older than me, and a picture of me. Both photographs taken from the same angle, at the same place.

Climbing up the mountain was not easy. It started with a hike along the La Mucuy route that lasted five days and included scaling the top of Pico Humboldt. I experienced fatigue, a lot of pain, hunger, cold, and insomnia. But the only thing that kept me moving forward was that photograph, the photo at the top of the mountain next to the liberator of my home country.

If I had focused on the process that would have been hell and that picture would have probably never been taken. There were plenty of moments when I felt like giving up. But the focus on the goal kept me fighting, looking forward to the long-awaited moment of standing next to the biggest bust of Bolivar I could have imagined along with the click of the camera. If the focus had been on the process it would have been hell, and the photograph would probably have never been taken because the times I could have called it quit were many.

4. It helps you to celebrate minor achievements. Being able to celebrate the minor achievements of a long journey will make all the difference. But the only way to be able to celebrate small advances is if you know where you are heading, and the only way to attain that is to write down your dreams and goals.

Near the end of 2012, I had the chance to meet Andres Gutierrez, a recognized US financial expert who has a radio program in which he offers personal financial advice. Andres has a foolproof plan designed to carry you from a life burdened with debt to a life of financial peace. One part of his plan is called the snowball. This concept has you list all your debts in order from least to greatest, not including your mortgage payment, and after making the minimum payments on all your debts, you vigorously attack the smallest one. After the smallest one is paid off, you add the payment that you used to make on that smallest debt to the second one. The moment you pay off the second one, you add that payment to the third one, and so on.

The system snowballs because as you pay down small debts your payment amount increases and you get to pay the larger ones faster.

However, in reality this is not the quickest way to get out of debt. The fastest way out of debt is to make a list of your debts from the one with the highest interest rate to the one with the lowest, then focus on paying the ones with the highest interest rate first.

Even though the system that focuses on interest rates is the one that would allow you to get out of debt more quickly and pay less, studies show that the system that Andres promotes is much more successful. Many more people get out of debt by organizing their debts from least to greatest than the people who organize them from highest interest to lowest. Why?

The reason is very simple. Getting out of debt is more than a financial issue or a math problem. It's an issue that involves our emotions. If people manage to eliminate one debt, even though it may be small, it gives them assurance, confidence in themselves, as well as motivation to continue with the second debt. When they manage to pay off the second one, this gives them even more motivation to go on to the third one. On the other hand, people trying to pay off debt for years, even though it has the highest interest rate, eventually lose motivation and quit.

This is Andres's motto: "Personal finances are more personal than financial." His secret to helping thousands of people get out of debt is leading them step by step through small victories, celebrating them, and then continue moving forward toward their ultimate goal.

> One of the best ways to attack a lack of motivation is to celebrate small successes.
> #innerherobook.com

The same thing happens with any other dream or goal in our lives. This is not a logical fight, we are in an emotional battle. And, as such we need to assure ourselves that we don't set ourselves up to be unmotivated. One of the best ways to attack a lack of motivation is to celebrate small successes. Did you jog for thirty minutes the first time without stopping? Celebrate. Did you play the first part of your favorite song without mistakes? Celebrate. Did you make your first sale? Celebrate.

However, when I say celebrate, I not talking about the kind of festivities that take place in my country that last for several days to commemorate the saints. I am referring to celebrating for five minutes and then keep moving forward with your goal. What you need is a small celebration, something that makes you feel rewarded for your small achievement.

So in closing this chapter, I want to share this with you. Every good film, the kind that is worth paying to go see in a theater, is born in the mind of someone. That someone wrote down the idea on a piece of paper. After that, they wrote the story, and then the script was developed. Always on a piece of paper.

Later on, someone else took the screenplay, and adapted it scene by scene. Others designed the costumes. Later on, the movie was filmed, edited, and sent to your local movie theater so you could see it.

But at the very beginning, what was born in someone's mind was written down on a piece of paper.

If you don't want life's windstorms to take your ship where you don't want to go, write down your dreams and goals. But defining your life's treasure is not the end of the battle.

In most cases, it is not even the beginning. At some point, every hero faces his first trial, and sometimes it's his most difficult. This is the reason why thousands return in fear to the ordinary world. This is the refusal of the call.

> If you don't want life's windstorms to take your ship where you don't want to go, write down your dreams and goals. #innerherobook.com

CHAPTER 7

THE REFUSAL OF THE CALL

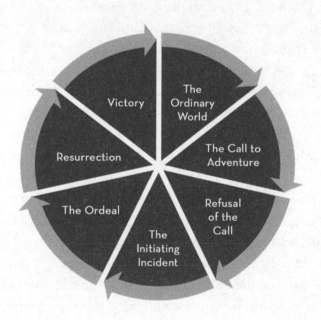

IT IS HARD TO PICK A FAVORITE movie or novel. Stories have different meanings for your life depending on when you see them and what you are going through at that moment in your life. Stories are not merely entertainment. They are an art form that gives us a window on the world as it should be. In the words of Robert McKee: "Good movies, novels, and plays that reflect all the tonalities of comedy and tragedy, always manage to amuse the audience by offering a new model of life laden with affective meaning. The stories are not an escape from reality but a vehicle that leads us in our search for reality, our best ally to give meaning to the anarchy of existence.[1]

One of my favorite movies is *The Hobbit*.[2] One scene in particular touched my heart powerfully at a stage of my life when I was between my ordinary world and a great story waiting to be written. I had already gotten the call to adventure, but I hadn't completely immersed myself in it yet.

I was denying my call.

In the first scenes of *The Hobbit*, Gandalf disrupts Bilbo's tranquility. Bilbo lives a quiet existence in a beautiful house in the shire. His life has become an ordinary world.

Gandalf has different plans. Without asking, he arranges a meeting at Bilbo's home to plan the next steps of his new adventure, to take back the lonely mountain that has been taken by Smaug the dragon. Bilbo is needed on this particular adventure and is invited to participate.

Bilbo, initially refusing to be part of the adventure, decides to read the contract he needs to sign in order to become part of the group. Once he delves into the details, here acts by loudly reading the risks: possible injury, evisceration, even incineration. Bilbo, not quite understanding how he might be incinerated, gets a clear answer from Bofur, who explains to him that the dragon that they will have to face could incinerate him in a blink of an eye.

As the risks of the adventure begin to sink in, taking a moment to get some fresh air, he faints with fear. After recovering, and sitting on his couch with a cup of hot tea, Bilbo has a conversation with Gandalf. It is one of the most powerful scenes of the story.

In this conversation Gandalf confronts Bilbo with the fact that he's lost his spirit of adventure. His mother's ornaments, carpets, and fine china had replaced the spirit that he had had when he was a little hobbit. A hobbit that was always looking to escape the bounds of the shire. Gandalf reminds him that life has to be lived and the world is outside, not inside, his home.

The conversation brings Bilbo a bit of hope and motivation. Nevertheless, before making the decision, he asks Gandalf if he can promise that he will return home safe and sound at the end of the adventure, to which Gandalf, unable to make such a promise, tells him no, but he points out to him that if he is successful in returning home, he will never be the same.

In that very moment, Bilbo stands up from the chair and leaves the room, warning Gandalf, "I will not go, you got the wrong hobbit!"

Going from the movie to the original book, I found an even more powerful description of what was going through Bilbo's mind and heart when he had that conversation with Gandalf:

> While they were singing, the hobbit felt within himself a love for beautiful hand-made, things – ingenious and magical – a wild and jealous love, the desire of the dwarves' hearts. Then, something of the Tuk was reborn in him. He wished to go out and see the huge mountains, to hear the pines and waterfalls, and to explore the caverns, and to carry a sword instead of a cane. He looked out the window. The stars where shining in the dark sky over the trees. He thought about the dwarves' jewelry that glittered in the dark caverns. Suddenly, a fire started in the woods beyond the water—maybe someone was lighting a fire—and he thought about devastating dragons that invaded the peaceful hill enveloping everything in flames. He shuddered and immediately became the simple Mr. Baggins again.[3]

Scenes like this represent key moments in our lives. Don't they? A friend tells us about a business that may just be able to give us the freedom we dream of. Someone tells us that we are excellent photographers, painters, or educators and a flame ignites inside of us that makes us hope, at least for a few seconds, that perhaps we could start doing something like that. Or we read an advertisement that promises to train us to become actors, singers, or comedians, and for a moment, something spiritual that we hadn't felt before fills us with new hope.

And it only takes a few seconds to consider the devastating dragons that envelop everything in flames, and once again we become the simple Mr. or Ms. Baggins.

I still remember like it was yesterday when I made the decision that starting my blog "liderazgohoy.com" was the way to obtain my dreams and respond to my call.

My mind was full of the possibilities that it could bring. I enthusiastically bought the domain and went ahead and paid for all of the services required to get the blog started. I had taken the first steps toward setting up this much-desired project.

I remember having gone to bed that night excited about what this project could become. But as I lay there in bed with everything in darkness and silence, I started to hear in my mind a very different narrative and one that began to dominate my thoughts: *What happens if this doesn't work? What happens if people don't like what I write? How about if I run out of subjects and have nothing more to say? Can you imagine how ashamed you'd feel around your friends and relatives if it doesn't work?*

All of my excitement and hope turned into fear, panic.

The next day, when I woke up, I cancelled all the services that I had signed up for. I asked them to give me my money back and a few hours later, I was calm again, with no lurking fears, and back in my ordinary world.

Fear, a feeling that we begin experiencing in childhood, can drown our lives in mediocrity. Fear in itself is not bad. The problem is how we interpret it and the actions we take as a consequence of fear.

The fears we experience in childhood are merely for our survival. After touching a hot stove or inserting a key in an electric socket (guilty!), you learned that in order to stay alive, you needed to keep your distance from those things. It was necessary to walk on the sidewalk after you ran out in the middle of the street and got spanked by your parents, avoid sticking your head out the window, etc. The problem is that we grew up believing that the only possible response to fear was to go back, withdraw, and avoid facing it.

And who better to teach us about fear than buffalos and cows?

Buffalos and cows react in completely different ways the moment they face one of their greatest fears: storms.

When cows see a storm on the horizon, they instinctively run away. They run in the opposite direction from where they see the storm coming. If they see the storm coming from the west, they turn around and run toward the east.

The problem is, because they are slow, cows are eventually overtaken by the storm. The moment they are overtaken, they keep running in the same direction. Because both the cows and the storm are heading in the same direction, this behavior only lengthens the time the cow is in the storm.

Believing they are running from the storm, they extend their time in it.

Buffaloes, on the other hand, behave differently. When a buffalo sees a storm on the horizon, he runs in the storm's direction. In spite of the fact that it doesn't seem to make any sense, at least for the cows, what happens is that when the storm and the buffaloes head in opposite directions, the latter manage to minimize their time in the storm.

Running away and avoiding fear is not our only response. We can can choose to face it.

Are you afraid? Let me assure you this is a good sign. Steven Pressfield, in his magnificent book, *The War of Art*, said, "The more afraid we are about a given project, the more certain we can be that the project is important for us and our soul's growth. That is the reason we feel so much resistance."[4]

Believe it or not artists, scientists, engineers, and anyone who considers himself a professional are always in search of activities and new horizons in their profession that incite fear. Real professionals are brave.

"The more afraid we are about a given project, the more certain we can be that the project is important for us and our soul's growth. That is the reason we feel so much resistance."
#innerherobook.com

Brave people are not the ones who have no fears, they are the ones who, in spite of having fears, face them. On the other hand, the amateur declines what frightens him. He prefers to keep himself safe and "successful" in his ordinary world.

> Brave people are not the ones who have no fears, they are the ones who face them.
> #innerherobook.com

Putting this book together made me terribly afraid. Especially today. As I am writing these lines, it has been a couple of months since I started it. In the process of developing the outline, laying out the chapters, and working on the publishing proposal, I made the decision to write this chapter that you are reading right now in a special moment.

I decided to write it in the moment I felt the most doubts, the most fears. I felt in order for me to write this chapter I needed to be immersed in the refusal of my call. I needed to be at that point at which my fears were convincing me that I wasn't going to make it.

If you are reading these lines, it means that I was able to overcome them, that I accepted my call to adventure.

I am sure you have faced circumstances like this one. What I mean is the moment when you are about to trade a future of adventure and risk for the safety that your ordinary world offers.

> Denying your call is a basic part of your development as a hero, and you need to go through that stage.
> #innerherobook.com

The point when you have to decide to fight for your dreams or devote your life to someone else's dreams for you, dreams imposed by society instead off dreams that were planted in your heart.

In the process I had to go through to understand the universal principles that make great stories and specifically the hero's journey, I understood something that gave me hope. Denying your call doesn't imply that you aren't a hero. On the contrary, it confirms it.

Denying your call is a basic part of your development as a hero, and you need to go through that stage. Every hero goes through a process of denial. It could be because you don't think you are capable, you're not "the chosen one," or because you don't want to leave the comforts of your ordinary world.

I have good news for your today! You are the chosen one in the great story of your life. You are its hero!

We need to understand that fear is a real feeling we have to learn to master and face bravely. Over time, I have developed certain steps and strategies that have helped me face fear. I want to share them with you.

1. Intentionally develop a positive intimate circle. There was a time, not long ago, when I realized that I hadn't been taking good care of my spiritual life. Something happened that made me slowly lose the habits and rituals that kept me in line with my Creator. That distancing, of course, was affecting other parts of my life, such as my marriage and my relationship with my son.

After a situation that will be the narrative of another book, I started a deep process of reflection to understand what had happened in my life that made me move away as I did. What had been the turning point of my spiritual life?

I thought for a while it had been my relocation from Venezuela to the US, and the fact that I had lost my church and had to go through a lot to find a new one here. But what I discovered is that my turning point, was when our prayer group broke up.

I was part of a group that met once a week to grow in knowledge about God and pray. I met excellent friends in that group whom I still visit and really appreciate.

Then the group split up. For good reasons, several of them had to leave from Venezuela. And, overnight we stopped meeting.

At the time, it wasn't a drastic change in my life. But I certainly lost a group of people overnight that used to help each other align themselves with God. As time passed, I didn't have that group to be accountable to, which allowed me certain flexibility that ended up in a major change from the person that I wished to become.

From that spiritual experience, which can be applied to any other area of your life, I drew the following conclusion. After God, no other area is as important to your future as the relationships you develop and the caliber of people with whom you spend your time.

John Maxwell always says in his conferences and books that in five years you will become the result of the average of your intimate circle.

If the people in your intimate circle generally have a great marriage, you will have a great marriage. If on average, they're financially free, eventually you will be as well. If, generally speaking, they're generous, you will become a generous person as well. Likewise, if the people in your intimate circle are negative, you will end up having a negative attitude. If your intimate circle is always badmouthing your spouse, you will most likely end up rejecting your wife or husband. If they spend more than what they make, you will end up with credit card collectors knocking on your door.

Another thing that I have learned in my life is that negative people will always try to destroy your dreams even though they call themselves your friends. They will always try to pull you into their negative, gossiping, and poisonous group. They'll do their best to keep you there. The fact that you have a call, a dream, is a threat to their basic existence. They can't allow you be successful because it will expose their negativity and lack of enthusiasm even more.

> Positive people have already left behind the ordinary world and are immersed in a story of adventure, risk, and victory, and they want you to experience it as well.
> #innerherobook.com

Positive people will move you forward. They will motivate you in the search of your dreams because they are looking for theirs too.

Positive people have already left behind the ordinary world and are immersed in a story of adventure, risk, and victory, and they want you to experience it as well.

The creation of an intimate circle with the people that you admire, with the kind of individuals that you would like to become, will be a constant source of support, motivation, and mentoring and will offer you unlimited opportunities.

2. I ask myself the question: *What happens if it works?* When you ask yourself this question, you set your mind in a different direction and show it a new perspective. When you ask yourself this question and give your imagination free rein, you bring out the deepest part of yourself and undertake one of the most important processes in the journey, visualization.

Charles Duhigg in his book *The Power of Habit* studied the process that made Michael Phelps the best swimmer in history and win more medals than anyone who has ever lived. In his book, he relates the following:

> Michael Phelps started swimming when he was seven to burn some energy because he was driving his parents crazy.
>
> A local trainer, Bob Bowman, realized that Phelps could go a long way. His body, long torso, relatively short legs and big hands—he was designed to become a great swimmer.
>
> But Phelps had a problem; he couldn't calm down before the competitions. He was very nervous.
>
> Bowman decided to give him something that would make him different: his competitive advantage. He taught Phelps the power of visualization.
>
> Every day, after his training, he used to tell him, "Don't forget to watch the video tonight and tomorrow morning, after you get up."
>
> The truth was that there was no video. Bowman meant that Phelps had to visualize the competition in his mind. Every night and every morning, Phelps used to close his eyes and visualize

himself jumping into the swimming pool, in slow motion, and swimming perfectly. He visualized each stroke, the turn, and the final goal.

Michael Phelps repeated "his video" thousands of times in his mind until he got to a point that when he was competing, he wasn't thinking. He simply followed a program. He had been programmed to win.

On August 13, 2008, at 10:00 in the morning, Michael Phelps dives into the pool to compete in the 200 meter butterfly stroke, one of his greatest strengths. As he enters the water, he knows that something is wrong: his swimming glasses are filling with water.

After a while, he can't see anything, not the line down the length of the pool or the "T" that shows the end. He doesn't know when to turn or finish. For most swimmers, this situation would lead them to panic and failure.

But not for Michael, he is calm.

Michael simply sticks to the program, "the mental video." He has already swum this competition many times in his mind and has won. He simply followed the program. Michael knows the number of strokes needed and when to turn. He is programmed to win.

That day, Michael Phelps not only won the gold in the competition but he broke the world record, all of this without even being able to see.

He remarked at the end of the competition: "It happened just the way I imagined it would. It was an additional victory in a life full of small victories."[5]

The power of visualization has made thousands of people attain their dreams. I will never forget my friend Rich Florence, who had had the opportunity to personally meet Evander Holyfield, one of the greatest boxers of all time. He told me that Evander used to read a list every of all the characteristics that he wanted to possess.

"Evander Holyfield?" I asked. "Evander Holyfield," he replied.

He showed me some of the things he had on his list. I remember reading very personal things about his spiritual life, but also things related to boxing like his speed, his strength, etc. If people like Evander Holyfield or Michael Phelps have for years used a power that is also at your disposal, don't you think it would be wise to take advantage of it?

Asking yourself what happens if your dream, goal, or call becomes reality will set you in the right direction and will provide your mind with what is needed to start the visualization process. Imagine what your life would look like if a business that you dream about starts to work out; what each day would hold you decide to embark on that trip across Europe that you've always dreamed of. Imagine how happy you would be if each day you dedicate the most important part of the day to doing what you're passionate about.

One of the secrets that I have discovered for turning the tables on fear and making it work to your advantage is to add the following questions to your visualization process. What would happen if you were actually going to be successful, but you never even tried? What would happen if your dream, idea, or passion was going to become a reality, but you never took the first step? That question sets fear to work to your advantage. Here is a great truth that I ask you to pay attention to. I prefer to face the pain of failure rather than the pain of regret. I prefer to try and fail, than wonder the rest of my life what would have happened if I had tried.

> I prefer to try and fail, than wonder the rest of my life what would have happened if I had tried. #innerherobook.com

One day, I made the decision that I preferred to come to the end of my life with a list of failures and a handful of victories, rather ending my days with a list of regrets because I never tried.

Never forget that the pain of failure goes away, but the pain of regret lasts a lifetime.

3. I ask myself the question: *What if it doesn't work out?* Like I said, fear itself is neither good nor bad. What is good or bad is the reaction we have when we face it. One of the most positive aspects of fear, which is linked to survival, is that it can guide you in a planning process to maximize your possibilities for success.

> Fear itself is neither good nor bad. What is good or bad is the reaction we have when we face it.
> #innerherobook.com

Many motivators and writers whose sole purpose is to sell speeches and books will tell you what you want to hear. Normally, it is something like this: *Go after your dreams, run after your passion, because if you do, everything will be all right, and you will be successful.*

I partially agree with statements like this. I do believe that you need to follow your call to adventure and identify your passion, but I don't believe that everything will necessarily be all right after you take the plunge. That is why it's of the utmost importance that you do the correct work of planning.

It was 1910 and two explorers, Robert Falcon Scott from England and Roald Amundsen from Norway, were competing to conquer one of the last uncharted areas of the earth, the South Pole.

The execution and results of these two expeditions were totally different. Amundsen got to the South Pole first and returned without major issues. Falcon arrived afterwards and was deeply disappointed when he saw Amundsen's flag already flying atop his goal. But the real tragedy happened later on when Falcon and his men died on the return at the base of the mountain due to fatigue, starvation, and exposure to the cold.

The big difference was planning. Falcon basically followed the path of one of his predecessors, Sir Ernest Shackleton, who, consequently, also never got to the goal and almost perished upon his return. Amundsen did his homework. He investigated alternative routes and studied ice growth patterns for years. This alternative route allowed him to build a base camp ninety-six kilometers closer to the goal, which meant a total savings of 193 kilometers of traveling.

Another big difference between the two of them was the methods of transportation. Falcon had some motorized machines, horses, dogs, and, of course, people. At the beginning of the expedition, he thought the dogs weren't the best idea and returned them to the base camp. Over time, he realized that the horses were unable work under such conditions, and they were all put down. The rest of the cargo was carried on foot.

On the other hand, Amundsen decided to only take dogs. Before the expeditions, he had learned survival techniques for extremely cold climates in order to prepare himself for this expedition. This is how he learned about the endurance of dogs. Dogs were excellent. They not only allowed him to advance eight to nine hours per day, compared with Falcon who could only move forward four or five, but warmed up the people and boosted the morale of the crew.

Falcon based all the preparations for his expedition on his predecessor, which gave him very little margin of error for unforeseen occurrences. Amundson left nothing to chance. He designed his glasses, skis, the dogs' harnesses, etc. These are some of the words of Roald Amundson:

> I may say that this is the greatest factor—the way in which the expedition is equipped—the way in which every difficulty is foreseen, and precautions taken for meeting or avoiding it. Victory awaits him who has everything in order—luck, people call it. Defeat is certain for him who has neglected to take the necessary precautions in time; this is called bad luck.[6]

Your desire to follow your call and begin the adventure of your life doesn't imply that you should be careless about planning and risk management. As the saying goes, "If you fail to plan, then you are planning to fail."

Asking, *What happens if it doesn't work?* has always helped me to define the worst-case scenario. If everything goes wrong, what are the consequences?

In most cases, I've noticed the consequences are not that serious. In cases where consequences were serious, it helps me to have a plan B, C, and, perhaps, D.

Here's a common example. Do you want to quit your job to pursue your dream? How about if you decrease your expenses to the minimum and save money over the next six to twelve months to have a financial cushion to support yourself if your business is taking more time than expected to grow? How about building your business or project in your free time, like nights and weekends, until the profit that comes from it replaces your present salary? Do you want to make a massive investment in a project or business? How about establishing an investment calendar where you have key dates that tell you if the progress meets your expectations or conversely, it is raises a red flag telling you to get out? Are you going to travel across country? How about making sure you have a spare tire? Anyway, the examples are endless. The point is you need to do your homework, you need to make a plan.

A clearly thought through action plan, with its respective cautions and back-up plans, will give your fears the most powerful death blow you could imagine.

> Fear is a negative feeling about something that hasn't happened. Your dream is a positive feeling for something that hasn't happened.
> #innerherobook.com

4. I spend time thinking about my dreams and goals. Some years ago, my friend Peter Blanco passed this thought on to me: "Fear is a negative feeling about something that hasn't happened. Your dream is a positive feeling for something that hasn't happened." In other words, what you fear and the dream are opposite sides to the same coin. Neither has happened yet. The fear is negative and the dream is positive.

That same day, Peter also told me, "Imagine a good dog and a bad dog. One of them represents fear, and the other one represents your dream. Which one will dominate? Which one will grow more powerful?

The one that you nurture most.

If you feed the dog of fear more—with negative people, stories of failure, etc.—it will grow and become so strong and powerful that will intimidate the other one. On the other hand, if you feed the dog of your dreams it will dominate your mind and won't leave room for fear in your life.

This is the reason why it is so important to dream. It is the most active process of visualization in which your dreams move from your mind and into the real world. Do you dream of becoming the conductor of an orchestra? Find a way to go to the most beautiful theater in your town, and one night, when it is empty, stand in the middle of the stage and conduct your most triumphant opus. Is it your dream to live in a particular place? Immerse yourself in pictures of the place that you pull from the Internet. Take a vacation and walk around its streets as if you were a resident. Are you there with family or a group of friends who are making fun of what you hope to achieve? Respectfully, remove yourself from their midst and go to the other side of the street and keep dreaming. Every day be intentional about choosing which dog you are going to feed.

5. I break down big projects into small tasks. One of the main reasons that fear rules us is because we see the task before us as one of such magnitude that we don't even know where to start much less believe that we will be able to finish it. The best strategy to attack this problem is to divide the project into the kind of small tasks that are extremely easy to accomplish.

Back in 2008, Procter & Gamble, the company that I work for, transferred me from Venezuela to its headquarters in Cincinnati, as a project manager of one of its biggest worldwide brands.

My job was to lead projects to launch new products to the market, to supervise the whole process and all its resources from the conception of the idea until the product hit the store shelves.

The first months were extremely difficult for me. Not only was I facing a new culture, a new country, and a new language, but I had never supervised projects of such magnitude. Just to give you an idea, the projects that I started managing meant investments of millions of dollars in the company, the purchase of equipment in our plants, very ambitious marketing plans, and countless processes needing to be qualified and approved to make sure that we were ready to launch to the market successfully.

There was a period of time that I was frightened. I even thought that I didn't have the skills to provide the results that were expected of me. To be totally honest, for a moment I thought that I could lose my job.

A few days later, I became convinced of something. I might not have the skills to manage a project of this magnitude, but I am capable of managing a small project.

What I decided to do was to break down all my projects into small tasks, such as *call Patricia in the Department of Research and Development to confirm that the formula passed the stability test,* or *go personally to meet the Head of Engineering to have an approval form signed to launch a product,* or *call X provider to make sure that the product was dispatched.*

What I mean is, it may be that I wasn't capable of managing a million-dollar project, but I certainly could call Patricia, go personally to the desk of the head of engineering, or confirm a delivery with a provider. Over time, I realized that by carrying out these small tasks, I was managing a gigantic project.

Break down your biggest projects into small tasks that are easy to carry out. You will see how when you start carrying out these small tasks that you will begin to build trust in

> Break down your biggest projects into small tasks that are easy to carry out.
> #innerherobook.com

yourself and to generate the necessary momentum to pursue your dreams. One day you will remember me, when without noticing, you are in the middle of your journey towards your dreams and have achieved things that you never believed possible. You will have beaten fear little by little.

These five steps have helped me tremendously in overcoming fear. And I am sure that they will be helpful to you as well.

The ordinary world is a place of high obstacles, protected by the soldiers of fear. But contrary to expectations, these soldiers of fear are not looking to protect you from dangers. Rather, they are preventing you from getting out. The soldiers of fear have become your jailers. They'll do everything possible to keep you from leaving the ordinary world.

> The soldiers of fear have become your jailers. They'll do everything possible to keep you from leaving the ordinary world. #innerherobook.com

Fear will use all its power to prevent you from living a great story and make you refuse your call. Fear knows that for every individual who is able to overcome it and live a fulfilled life, it will become weaker and weaker. Taking the plunge and deciding to live the life of your dreams will not only bless you but will inspire others who are ruled by fear.

Although, like it or not, there will be moments that, intentionally or accidentally, will force you into your story. There are moments when we face an initiating incident.

> Taking the plunge and deciding to live the life of your dreams will not only bless you but will inspire others who are ruled by fear. #innerherobook.com

CHAPTER 8

THE INITIATING INCIDENT

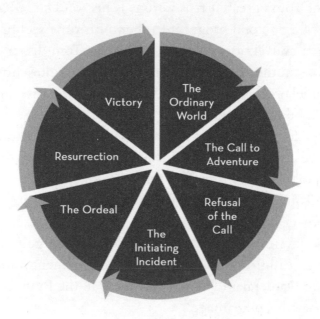

ONE OF THE MOVIES THAT has touched my heart is *The Way*.[1] It portrays the transformative experience of Tom Avery, an ophthalmologist who, by a twist of fate, decides to embark on an adventure he'd never himself dreamed of, walking the Camino de Santiago.

The Camino de Santiago is a spiritual pilgrimage that thousands of people take every year. There are several routes, but one of the main ones starts in the French Pyrenees and covers a distance of more than eight hundred kilometers to get to where it is believed the remains of the Apostle James are located..

I have a good friend, Stewart Marquina, who made the trip some years ago and told me that it was a spiritual experience that changed his life.

But Tom Avery's story doesn't begin there. It starts in his ordinary world as a successful ophthalmologist whose life has sunk into one of boredom since the death of his wife. Without much detail, we infer that his life is predictable, calm, and safe. A life that fluctuates between his office and the golf course. The death of his soul can be detected from a great distance.

One of Tom's greatest frustrations is his son Daniel's decision to drop out of a doctoral program to spend his time seeing the world. In fact, in a conversation that takes place as Tom drives him to the airport for another one of his trips, Daniel invites him to come along. Daniel promises his father a father-son adventure, an excursion that would be unforgettable.

As expected, Tom gives his son a series of explanations why he wouldn't be able to leave town for such a long time and drops Daniel at the airport to start his new adventure alone.

What Tom doesn't know is that an unexpected event will change his life forever.

A few days later, in the middle of one of his golf games, Tom gets a phone call from the French police department informing him that his son Daniel has died in an accident in the Pyrenees as he was about to start his pilgrimage.

Tom immediately leaves for France in order to pick up his son's body. As a tribute and out of grief for his son, he decides to travel the ancient spiritual way where his son died carrying his ashes with him.

I remember a scene in which, his journey well underway, he awakes to have a hostel owner stamp his passport for him. He asks her:

"Have you ever done the way?"

"Never," she replies, "Never. When I was younger, I was very busy, and now I am old and tired."[2]

The Camino de Santiago changes Tom's life. In the process, he makes some friends who together are looking to find more meaning in their lives. Tom's adventure along the way leads him to a deep spiritual relationship with his son, whom, in my opinion, he finally gets to know.

After arriving at their destination of Santiago de Compostela, Tom travels to Muxia with three of his new friends to scatter his son's ashes at sea.

The movie finishes with Tom readying himself for a new adventure, carrying Daniel's backpack.

Just as Titanic is about Rose's freedom, Tom's story is also about his freedom. Being set free from an ordinary world. His son's death was an event that forces Tom into the story, in the same way that Scott Harrison of charity: water needed to hit bottom to wake up, or Bilbo needed to be confronted by Gandalf to decide to join the adventure.

Each story needs what we could call the initiating incident. It is the turning point of all great stories. It is an event that forces the hero to move; it forces the character to enter into the story. It like is a door of no return. After that moment, nothing will be the same. Don Miller describes it as follows, referring to Robert McKee in his book *The Script*:

> It is the turning point of all great stories. It is an event that forces the hero to move; it forces the character to enter into the story.
>
> #innerherobook.com

Robert McKee says that we humans, by nature, look for comfort and stability, and with no initiating incident to disturb us, we won't get into the story. We have to get fired from work or be forced to sign up for a marathon. There is a ring that we have to buy or a house we need to sell. The character has to throw himself into the story, into discomfort and fear, otherwise, the story won't ever happen.[3]

Each initiating incident happens differently for each story. If we could place them in two groups, there would be ones that happen externally, outside of our circle of influence, and those that happen internally, inside our circle of influence.

Initiating incidents external to our circle of influence are the stories like Tom's in *The Way,* or getting fired from work, or being diagnosed with an illness. They are events that not only leave a mark but rock our lives. They are circumstances that—when they happen—eliminate almost instantly all the dirt and the fog in our lives and, through extreme feelings like pain or happiness, show us clearly what's really important in our lives.

This kind of external initiating incident is not necessarily negative. As in most cases, it is connected to death, disease, or crisis in general. It also happens to some people in moments of extremely positive experiences. In which case the result is difficult to explain without using words like *miracle* or *supernatural.* These are often cases of deep spiritual enlightenment.

I have friends who made drastic decisions in their lives because they are deeply convinced that God healed them or healed a loved one. They had a positive experience in their lives that they consider to be divine intervention and that led them to change the course of their story.

One of the most striking stories is that of Paul who was leading the persecution of the Christian church. Paul had a divine encounter that led him to completely change the trajectory of his life to become one of the greatest leaders ever known.

Whether or not you believe in Paul's divine encounter is totally irrelevant. The event was so powerful that it led Paul to suffer hunger, imprisonment, and a great deal of pain. Regardless of whether you believe the details of his conversion, the reality is that it radically changed his life and transformed him into one of the greatest leaders of the Christian church, and that's what counts.

What I am trying to tell you is that the initiating incident is the event that is important to you, not to other people. It's the event that shakes your world, not necessarily that of others. It may be that you are the only one who believes in it and that is okay.

Many times we are in search of this kind of initiating incident. We want an angel to appear before us and throw us onto the floor in his great power and show us our destiny. But like I said before, this kind of initiating incident is outside our circle of influence, and for this reason, we cannot wait for one of them to start living a great story.

Which brings me to the next question. Setting aside positive transforming experiences like Paul's miraculous healing and leaving only the painful ones, would you really want to wait for something extreme to happen in order to move you? Is it so wonderful to be on the couch all day long watching TV that you need a sickness, the death of a loved one, or an extreme crisis to push you to have a life worth living?

It's important to answer this question. Unfortunately, I have met many people like this who, perhaps unconsciously, are waiting for a tragedy to do something inspiring with their lives. You don't necessarily need to lose your legs to make up your mind to run have marathon. You don't need to declare bankruptcy to help others improve their personal finances. You don't need to have a terminal illness to inspire others to live. If life has dealt you these blows or others, and you have decided to transform them into an inspiration, I take my hat off to you. But, if not, you don't need to wait for that. You can start living an inspirational life now. You can force the initiating incident to happen.

Just as there is an external initiating incident outside of your circle of influence, there is also an internal initiating incident or one that is within your circle of influence. Here is where you can make a difference.

Donald Miller, whom I mentioned at the beginning of this book, grew up without a father. His father abandoned him at a young age his mother never talked about him. But his mother's silence never extinguished Don's deep need to understand who he was. By understanding his father, he would understand his own story a little more.

In his book, *A Million Miles in a Thousand Years*, Don confesses:

> I didn't want to have to tell him who I was, without having accomplished some kind of physical achievement related to athletics, even remotely. And I think that the fact that I never had to get together with him, helped me forgive him also. Without the concern of what would his opinion be about me, I could assume that he always wanted to contact me and maybe he secretly watched me once in a while. Perhaps he looked at me at a distance from some field while I was rehearsing in the band. The day I graduated from high school, I remember wondering if he might be in the stands, and I felt his eyes watching me, and I was frightened by the idea, even then, of seeing him emerge from the shadows.[4]

Despite his desire to meet his father, Don never looked for him. Every time he felt restless again (the call to adventure), fear soon took control and dominated (refusal of the call). But one day, something happened.

Don got a phone call from his mother who invited him to meet his father. After apologizing for never having talked about him, she confessed that she had gotten some papers with his address and phone number. Don had received a new call to adventure. About this, he says:

> I kept driving to my friend's house and when I stopped the car and put my fingers on the handle of the door to get out, I started shaking. I was short of breath. I couldn't understand my emotions yet, but without a doubt, I was feeling something. I entered the house, and I suspect the people thought I was on drugs – because I hardly talked....
>
> I had his phone number in my wallet, but I didn't call him. A month passed, but I didn't call him, and another month. I had

planned a trip to Chicago and I told myself that when I went, I would call him and go to Indiana to meet him. Nevertheless, the first night I didn't call him, and the second night I didn't either. So my last day arrived and I knew I had to do something. I knew that I needed an inducting incident, something that would obligate me to get into the story. Then I sent a text message to ten of my friends, telling them that I would get together with my father, whom I hadn't seen in thirty years.[5]

Don was consumed with fright at meeting his father almost for the first time. He needed an initiating incident, and sending those text messages to his friends was what occurred to him. He knew that when he got back home, all his friends would ask him about his father, and he couldn't tell them he had been a coward. The initiating incident, created by him, forced him to get into the story, forced him to overcome fear and live the adventure.

> The initiating incident that is in your circle of influence is the event that you create to force yourself to get into the story.
> #innerherobook.com

The initiating incident that is in your circle of influence is the event that you create to force yourself to get into the story. It is when you stop by the jewelry store and finally decide to buy the engagement ring. It's when you register at the gym. It's when you tell everyone that this year you will run the marathon. The ability to create an initiating incident is the difference between brave people and cowards. While cowards turn back to their ordinary world and hide, brave

> The ability to create an initiating incident is the difference between brave people and cowards.
> #innerherobook.com

people commit themselves to their story by generating an initiating incident.

Although there are initiating incidents of great magnitude and impact such as the death of a loved one, an illness, or a marriage engagement, there can be smaller ones such as a text message to a friend or a commitment in front of coworkers. The main goal of the initiating incident is to overcome inertia.

> The main goal of the initiating incident is to overcome inertia.
> #innerherobook.com

Physics is a fascinating science that has always captured my attention. It explains inertia as the property bodies have to remain in the same state, resting or moving, as long as the difference between the force applied and the resistance is zero. The force necessary to take an object from its state of rest or to change its moving trajectory has to be greater than the resistance. In other words, it needs to overcome inertia.

Have you ever let go of your bicycle handlebar while moving? Even though at first you were probably afraid, you must have noticed that the handlebar kept itself perfectly aligned without moving to one side or the other, and with no need to hold it. Why? Because of inertia. The bike, every particle of it, wants to keep itself moving in its original direction until an external force, for example, a rock, takes it out of its original trajectory—and is the reason you fell and skinned your knees.

> The main goal of the initiating incident is to take you out of a state of rest or change your direction.
> #innerherobook.com

Why do you think that successful people become more and more successful while others don't? Inertia. When a body is moving, it will keep moving until an external force changes its direction.

That external force is the initiating incident. The main goal of the initiating incident is to take you out of a state of rest or change your direction. Like I mentioned before, it could be something big, but it could also be small things that start the process of overcoming inertia.

This is the reason why in the previous chapter I recommend breaking down big projects into small tasks. When huge projects paralyze you, simple and small tasks will help you overcome inertia. The idea of opening your dream business, where you sell the most beautiful dresses anywhere, may be a task that paralyzes you. But, buying the newspaper or checking on the Internet for commercial property for rent is a much easier thing to do. Remember, you are overcoming inertia.

Breaking down your project into small tasks, taking baby steps, sending a text message to your friends, will help you overcome inertia. But I have to be honest with you, the moment will come when you'll need to take a specifics step that plunges you into the story, a step that commits you, the real door of no return. It is when you move from safety to risk, when you deliver the engagement ring, when you quit your job in order to dedicate yourself full time to your personal project. It is when you knock at your father's door after not seeing him for thirty years. It's not simply when you take action, but when you take the one action that plunges you into the story definitely. That moment will arrive and you have to be prepared.

Sometimes people ask me why I use so many movies to explain the principles that make great stories, but leave novels aside somewhat. One reason is that I watch more movies than I read novels. But that isn't the main reason. The real reason is this. In a novel, you can easily distinguish facts from thoughts. You can draw a line between intention and action. You can be reading a novel where a character, in spite of loving his wife deeply, decides to have a one-night stand with another woman. Or another character may think about doing wrong to someone, but nevertheless, behave in a different way.

In a movie it is different. Movies normally can't communicate intention, only action. If you want the audience to perceive a character as a generous one, the character needs to show an act of generosity. If you want the audience to perceive him as fearful, he or she has to run away from a situation in a cowardly way. If you want him to be a hero, he needs to overcome fear and throw himself into the story in some real way. He has to take action, not simply have an intention.

If you remember Bilbo Baggins's story in *The Hobbit*, there is a significant difference between the book and the movie for the same scene. In the book, all Bilbo's struggles are internal, "While they were singing, the hobbit felt in himself a love for beautiful things handmade with creativity and magic; a fierce and jealous love, the dwarves' heart's desire. Then something about the Tuk was reborn in himself..."

And the refusal of his call was also internal, "...and he thought about devastating dragons that invaded the peaceful hill, wrapping everything in flames. He trembled and immediately became the simple Mr. Baggins again."[6]

In contrast, when the movie was made, they had to alter this scene into a conversation between Gandalf and Bilbo because, like I said before, movies do not convey intention, just action.

And I like that. I believe at the end of our lives what matters is our actions, not our intentions. I don't want to be remembered by people as the man who wanted to be a good husband and parent who wanted to be honest, who wanted to be self-controlled who wanted to follow God. I want to be remembered for what I did. In the end, what matters is action, not intention.

> I believe at the end of our lives what matters is our actions, not our intentions.
> #innerherobook.com

I want to refer again to Steven Pressfield's words about the power of taking action:

If tomorrow, by some twist of fate, each and every one of those souls were to wake up with the power to take the first step toward accomplishing their dreams, all the psychiatrists around the world would be unemployed. The prisons would be empty. The alcohol and tobacco industries would close down, along with the junk food, plastic surgery, and advertising industries, not to mention the pharmaceutical companies. Domestic violence would be over as well as addictions, obesity, migraines and dandruff problems.[7]

Living a great story isn't easy. What's easy is left behind in the ordinary world. Living a great story has much more to do with adventure, risks, battles, and victories, of fulfillment and life more than searching for what's easy and taking the path of least resistance.

The initiating incident plunges you into the story it is in that process when we make one of our biggest mistakes. A mistake that has to do with expectations more than anything else. We think that leaving the ordinary world to follow our call to adventure is the climax of the story. We think that quitting our job, or placing the engagement ring on our loved one's finger, signing up for the marathon, or yelling to the world that we have decided to quit an addition is the climax. But it is not.

The problem with this confusion is that by believing that the initiating incident is the climax, we then won't understand the reason for all the obstacles, battles and conflicts that we are about to face. The climax takes place after the hero's resurrection. Later. Not when he first decides to throw himself into the story.

> Living a great story isn't easy. What's easy is left behind in the ordinary world.
> #innerherobook.com

In the same way that the initiating incident plunges you into the adventure, it also plunges you into conflict, which will be responsible for changing your life forever.

PART THREE

THE ORDEAL

CHAPTER 9

CONFLICT AND RESISTANCE

THINK FOR A MOMENT about your favorite movies, those that have touched your heart, and you will find a common element in all of them: great conflict. Conflict is what makes a story a worthy one.

> Conflict is what makes a story a worthy one.
> #innerherobook.com

Can you imagine *Rocky* with no fights? Or *Star Wars* without the forces of evil? Or a love story like *Meet Joe Black* without the tension caused by Joe as death itself? Or Disney movies with no dragons, spells, or cruel stepmothers? Every story breathes with life and inspiration through conflict. Real life is no different.

Your life story will be as interesting as the level of conflict that you are willing to overcome. Period.

> Your life story will be as interesting as the level of conflict that you are willing to overcome.
> #innerherobook.com

What I mean is that you no longer have to wonder, *Why does this happen to me?* But rather to understand that battles, conflicts, failures, and obstacles are there to make your life a more interesting story, one of those that is worth living and telling.

> Battles, conflicts, failures, and obstacles are there to make your life a more interesting story, one of those that is worth living and telling.
> #innerherobook.com

In the world of stories, movies, and novels they are called opposing forces. They are the forces that work against the hero in accomplishing his goal. They're forces that want to keep you in the ordinary and prevent you from stepping out and living your adventure. And if you do step out, they work strongly to bring you to a level of frustration so high that you refuse the call and return to the safety of your ordinary world.

The best representation of these forces can be seen in the movie *Star Wars*, where the dark force is constantly at work against the forces of good. That is why they have the motto, *May the force be with you.*

I believe we live in a world where true antagonistic forces are at work. The natural process of human development doesn't take him to fulfillment and success. On the contrary, it sinks him in misery. We live in a world like the one in *Star Wars* where there is a force that is trying to destroy our soul and neutralize us.

If you don't believe me, simply put it to the test. Sit down for lunch with your coworkers and tell them that you have decided to follow your dreams, and you will see how laughs and envy begin to blossom; or make up your mind to bring an idea to the market and watch how, in your first attempts, everything that could go wrong will or decide that you are going to leave being overweight behind, and in only a few days you'll realize how hard it is to commit to.

Have you ever seen a good addiction? Why do people only develop addictions to bad things? Have you ever thought about it?

I have never met anyone addicted to generosity, broccoli, or tofu. Even the people who are addicted to activities such as exercise take the activity to the point where it is detrimental to their life, their relationships and even their physical health. People don't get addicted to the good or to good things. People get addicted to sugar, carbohydrates, alcohol, drugs, promiscuity, etc.

The reason is this. There is an opposing force that wants to destroy you, to neutralize you.

One of the main opposing forces that you will face is resistance. Resistance is that force which, according to the concept of inertia I explained in the previous chapter, wants to keep you in a state of rest. Resistance is what prevents your vehicle from going downhill by itself when you park it on a slope or what allows an airplane to stop before it reaches the end of the runway. But, it is also the force that will keep you anchored to your couch. It's the force that will pat you on the back when you decide to watch your favorite TV show instead of starting to write that book that you've dreamed of. It will tell you, *You deserve it, you're tired.*

> Resistance is that force which, according to the concept of inertia I explained in the previous chapter, wants to keep you in a state of rest.
> #innerherobook.com

Have you ever committed to work out, to write a book, or wake up every morning to pray only to realize it's not only difficult but almost impossible to get out of bed? Have you ever made the decision to eat healthy only to notice that precisely that week your coworkers bring cake and doughnuts? Or have you ever decided that definitely you were going to honor the love for your wife and stop looking at all pornography on the Internet only to notice that, as you're changing the channel on your television, a Victoria's Secret commercial comes on? Let me introduce to you resistance.

Steven Pressfield, in his book *The War of Art* has written one of the best manifestos that I have come across regarding resistance. He writes:

> Resistance is the most toxic force on the planet. #innerherobook.com

Resistance is the most toxic force on the planet. It causes more sadness than poverty, disease and erectile dysfunction. Surrender to Resistance distorts our spirit. It paralyzes us and make us less than what we are and what we are destined to be. If you believe in God, you have to recognize the malignant character of Resistance, because it doesn't allow us attain the life that God has reserved for us when He gave our genius to each of us...

What is particularly insidious about the justifications that resistance offers us is that many of them are true and legitimate. Our wife really may be in her eighth month of pregnancy; she really may need us at home. Our work department really may be establishing a change in the schedule that will take hours away from our day. It really may make sense to procrastinate our thesis, at least until the baby is born.

What resistance doesn't tell us, of course, is that all of this means nothing. Tolstoy had thirteen children and even so he wrote *War and Peace*. Beethoven was deaf and even so, he used to write symphonies.

If Resistance couldn't be defeated, the Fifth Symphony wouldn't exist, nor *Romeo and Juliet* or the Golden Gate Bridge. Defeating Resistance is like giving birth. It seems completely impossible until you remember that women have been doing it successfully, with or without help, for about fifty million years.[1]

Resistance can be beaten only with action. Resistance will manipulate your feelings like you can't imagine: it will make you feel that you've lost your love for your wife or husband; it will make you feel like you have nothing to write; it will convince you putting off your project one more day won't cause any problems; it will invite you to stay in the warmth of your sheets one more morning. The big problem is that many people don't know that this opposing force exists, and consequently, they think it's simply the way to live life.

The reality is that if you want to do something great with your life, you need to convince yourself that you have an enemy that is trying to neutralize you. And only by taking a step forward and acting you will be disarming it and taking away all its power.

> Resistance can be beaten only with action.
> #innerherobook.com

About twelve years ago, I read a book called *The Richest Man in Babylon*. In it, the author explains that a person should save ten percent of everything they earn. The concept seemed interesting to me and I decided to apply it. It was simple for the first few months, but over time, a problem here or there, a trip that I wanted to make or a toy that I "needed" to buy, led me to neglect it and finally forget about it.

Ten years later, I was talking to a co-worker with whom I had developed a friendship. In our conversation we touched on the subject of our retirement plans, and he confessed that he had saved more than two hundred fifty thousand dollars. I was impressed and probably assuming that it had been a present from a family member, asked him what he had done to save all that money, and he replied, "A few years ago, I read a book called *The Richest Man in Babylon*. I highly recommend it. It talks about saving ten per cent..."

There I was, sitting in front of a person my same age, working in the same company as me, at the same management level, the same size family. The only difference was that he had defeated resistance, while resistance was telling me, *Calm down, you will save next month. Your car needs a new stereo. Enjoy today; don't worry about tomorrow. You totally deserve it.* It was telling him the exact same things it was telling me. The difference wasn't in the resistance, it was in the action.

The most powerful movies I have watched are those that present the hero with a dilemma. Why? Because the choice between good and evil is not really a difficult choice, it is trivial. The dilemma comes when the hero has options, each one with positive and negative aspects. Why does *Star Wars: Episode VI—Return of the Jedi* have a much more powerful end than the previous one? Because in *Star Wars: Episode IV* Luke Skywalker destroys the Death Star (a decision between good and evil, not really a difficult decision), while in *Star Wars: Episode V* the very moment Luke is about to finish off Darth Vader, he confesses that he is Luke's father. In that moment, Luke faces a dilemma. Should he finish off the epicenter of evil, and in doing so kill his father? Or should he feel compassion for the father who gave him life, but allow evil to survive? This is a dilemma. This is the "end of a movie." Dilemmas like this have created powerful stories. Movies like *The Godfather* are a dilemma, series like *Breaking Bad* are born out of a dilemma. And we need to understand that we will constantly face dilemmas like these.

> The dilemma comes when the hero has options, each one with positive and negative aspects.
> #innerherobook.com

One of the most powerful features of resistance is that it always presents itself in the form of a dilemma. It doesn't tell you, *Stay in bed and rest and throw your dreams in the trash.* It will always present itself to you in the form of a dilemma, *You deserve to rest. Rest will refresh your mind. Tomorrow you will be fresh and more productive.* Or, *It doesn't matter if you don't have the money. Borrow some. Life is for living today, not tomorrow. You'll be able to pay it off with no problem.* Resistance, clever force, will always present itself to you in the form of a dilemma.

> One of the most powerful features of resistance is that it always presents itself in the form of a dilemma.
> #innerherobook.com

Thousands of years ago, others wrote about this force. The Scriptures talk about Satan, George

Lucas calls it the "forces of evil," and Steven Pressfield calls it "resistance." What you call it doesn't make any difference. What's important is that you know that it exists and that it doesn't want to see you get up.

When I started studying at the university I worked at a summer camp during my summer vacation. The camp was held on a dream ranch, one of the most beautiful places I've ever visited.

Some days, I used to venture out on my bike with the boys from my cabin over the savannahs and never-ending plains of that unforgettable place. We would lose ourselves for hours cutting new paths for ourselves because taking the paths that already existed bored us. We discovered new rivers and lagoons, the remains of a dead cow, and came across a few dangerous wild animals. Because the ranch was so big and to avoid getting lost, I decided to always guide myself by the sun. In the morning, I ventured to the west and returned in the afternoon in an eastward direction. I used to do it that way in order to always have the sun at my back. I knew that if the sun was behind me, I was going in the right direction. In other words, if we stopped to chat and rest, when we needed to resume riding, I simply looked at the sun, turned my back to it and started to pedal.

I see resistance in the same way, and I understand that I always need to have it at my back and strain in the opposite direction. Resistance has become to me the way to confirm whether my path is the right one. When I feel that it is pushing me in one direction, I push in the opposite direction. It's that simple.

You need to become acquainted with resistance. You need to learn to recognize its voice, you need to learn to detect its steps when it's coming toward you. You need to learn how to decode its lies, so that the moment it comes at you, you can see it as a confirmation that you are on the right path and need to take action.

Resistance has become to me the way to confirm whether my path is the right one.
#innerherobook.com

CHAPTER 10

CONFLICT AND ITS BEAUTY

WHEN WE ARE IN THE MIDDLE OF CONFLICT, all we see is darkness, but the reality is that it is preparing us for something big. We are creating a story that is worth telling.

The bigger our project, dream, or call, the more conflict we'll have to overcome. It is a universal rule of life. Small dreams will have small conflicts; big dreams, big conflicts, failures, and obstacles.

> Small dreams will have small conflicts; big dreams, big conflicts, failures, and obstacles.
> #innerherobook.com

But conflict results in something beautiful, something worthwhile. The focus shouldn't have to be on the conflict, but on what you will become in the process. That is your greatest gift. In the same way that an athlete pays a high price year after year for the opportunity to stand with an Olympic medal aorund his neck, we need to do so as well. There is a medal out there that will be delivered to you only when you pass the test, after you face conflict.

There are countless benefits to conflict. Here are some of them.

1. Conflict helps you appreciate life itself. I grew up in Venezuela. This country has one of the best climates in the world. Caracas, the city where I grew up, is always sunny, with a climate around eight-six degrees throughout the year. I remember going to the beach any time of the year. Regardless of whether it was December or July—it was always perfect.

> The focus shouldn't have to be on the conflict, but on what you will become in the process. That is your greatest gift.
> #innerherobook.com

I had been there since I was a baby, so I always thought that climate was normal, so I took it for granted. Having good weather was the expected climate. That was the way it was. Period. When I moved to Cincinnati, I found myself facing a reality I never expected, an infernal winter. Temperatures of forty degrees below zero or worse, for months. Sometimes I went for weeks without seeing the sun, which was always hidden by a thick layer of gray clouds that, without noticing, led you to depression. Then there's wearing coats that weighed pounds, not to mention hitting a patch of black ice in your car, frequent accidents, the dreadful cold, battling with snow just so you can walk, and worst of all, being shut up indoors for nearly five months.

But as they say, nothing lasts forever. Eventually the cold ends and spring arrives.

I remember one day when I was getting ready to go to work when out of the blue I heard some birds singing. "Did you hear that?" I asked my wife. What happens is that during the winter time you don't hear any birds singing, and after several months you get used to the silence of the season. But when spring arrives, you begin to appreciate that sound again.

And not only the sound of the birds, I also remember beginning to appreciate the days we had a clear blue sky. Simply beholding the sun becomes something beautiful, like a miracle. If you add some warmth, a refreshing breeze, the birds, and a good meal cooked on the barbecue out in the open air, you felt like you were literally in heaven.

What is odd about this is that I had the warmth, the refreshing breeze, the outdoor barbecue, and the birds in Venezuela all my life, every day, but because they were commonplace, I took them for granted.

Have you ever had fractured a bone or cut your finger? I'm sure it affected everything you needed to do but could no longer do because of the temporary disability. All of them were activities that you took for granted.

A person who has had a profound impact on me is Tony Melendez. Tony was born with no arms. One day, he fell in love with a guitar that his father had, but he never thought about what the future had in store for him. His father raised him to be an independent man and never allowed his son to use his disability to make excuses. Tony says that his father always told him, "Tony, you have to try. You have to do it by yourself. "

He always had a passion for music. His mother used to sing and his father played the guitar. Tony, with no arms, would practice six to seven hours a day until it resulted in music. In 1987, he played a beautiful song to Pope John Paul II in front of thousands of people all over the United States.

Tony Melendez says that people ask him why he feels so complete and he responds, "Because I have these (referring to his legs) that can do everything. I have my precious family, my heart wants to dance, to sing and, to live my life because in God's eyes, I am complete."

Later on during his interview, he says, "I see people like you that have arms, feet, and everything, and they say I can't, I can't... they can, they can! I have been asked, 'Where are the miracles?' And I always say this: When I see a hand, I see a miracle."[1]

Being born with no arms combined with the constant everyday struggles Tony has had to face his whole life, has led him to appreciate life at a level that probably few have.

Every day thousands of people wake up and start their daily routines without appreciating life itself unfolding before their eyes: the weather, the birds, the aroma of coffee, legs, arms, health, sun, rain, your children's faces, the smile of a stranger, the simple fact of being alive.

Conflict reawakens all of that. Conflict gives you back the life that routine and day-to-day activities steal from you. Conflict opens your eyes to a new level. Conflict helps bring you back to life.

2. **Conflict helps you evolve.** Ask any successful person what were the key moments of their lives that shaped them to become the person they are today, and most of them will talk about their conflicts, their obstacles, and their failures.

> Conflict helps bring you back to life.
>
> #innerherobook.com

Nobody flourishes in a Jacuzzi in a hotel in Hawaii while getting a back massage. There's nothing wrong with this. In fact, I would love to have a back massage while drinking a piña colada in a Jacuzzi in Hawaii. But the reality is that those are not moments of growth. Moments like these are beautiful, moments of celebration, rest, restoration and enjoyment, but normally, these are not the moments that will bring out the best in you. That is reserved for conflict.

The best movies clearly show the hero evolve and how conflict affects him and helps him grow. In Lord of the Rings, we can see how Frodo, Pippin, Merry, and Sam start the adventure as a group of immature and cowardly friends, but because of an external initiating incident, they are forced to enter into the story.

As the story unfolds their characters change and they develop leadership and courage. The adventure to destroy the ring changes them. They will never be the same. Their evolution has gone from heaven to earth. Now they are totally different hobbits.

Conflict changes you. People who don't understand that conflict is a necessary process of evolution, can develop negative characteristics like cynicism, frustration, and even depression. But the ones who understand the purpose of conflict simply take advantage of it to get the best of themselves and come out of conflict a more complete and fulfilled individual.

One of the most admirable qualities I've seen in high level executives and entrepreneurs is their instinct. I've always been impressed with how, in spite of trends, data, or any information you may give them, they follow their instinct in an almost spiritual way, and in most cases, they are successful.

Trying to learn from them, I asked a high-level executive from General Electric about the subject, who told me the following story.

A reporter asks a high-level executive the secret to his success. The executive replies:

"Four words: Make the right decisions."
"How do I learn to make the right decisions?" the reporter asks.
"Four words. Get the right experience."
And then the reporter asks the last question.
"How do I get the right experience?"
The executive responds:
"Four words: Make the wrong decisions."

Instinct, the ability to make a decision based on a gut feeling and many times not supported by logic, is developed through conflict. You need to make mistakes to learn how to do it well.

I once heard Rob Bell say the following referring to the power of conflict to produce growth and change:

I can assure you that the people that have impacted you the most, those you admire the most, and the kind of person you would like to become, I assure you that they are people who have suffered, because nobody gets a free pass.

I can assure you they are people who, in the midst of suffering, consciously or unconsciously, made decisions to become a particular kind of person in order to let the event shape them, and they didn't try to get out of suffering, but they allowed themselves to go through this process and come out on the other side.

And when people choose to live that way, when they trust that, despite the fact that this can feel like death, resurrection is coming; when people choose to live with that kind of confidence it changes everything.[2]

> Many times we make the mistake of seeing conflict as a sign that the world is coming to an end, when it is really a sign that the world is changing. #innerherobook.com

Many times we make the mistake of seeing conflict as a sign that the world is coming to an end, when it is really a sign that the world is changing. Great conflicts have brought tremendously positive things that demonstrate our evolution as a —the establishment of human rights, the abolition of slavery, racial equality, democracy, and much more. When societies go through profound conflicts their individuals need to believe in this transformation and not be overcome by the conflict. Rather, they should face it with the conviction that this process, albeit painful, is leading them to a better world.

> From the darkest moments come the most beautiful stories, ventures, and projects. #innerherobook.com

I want to be sensitive about this point. I understand that you may possibly be going through an extremely difficult ordeal, and there's only silence and darkness all around you, I understand. I've been there and done that. And when you are in the middle of darkness, it's difficult to understand why such difficult events happen. Divorce, death, illness, bankruptcy, rape, slavery. I presume within these lines to take God's place and try to convince you the reason for every conflict is to help you evolve as an individual. The truth is that there are many cases I don't understand either. What I can assure you of is that conflict will bring something good out of you, if you let it. From the darkest moments come the most beautiful stories, ventures, and projects. From the darkest moments, the greatest blessings to mankind come about. The darkest hour is just before the dawn.

> The darkest hour is just before the dawn.
> #innerherobook.com

3. Conflict helps you connect with others through pain. Years ago, I traveled to Columbus, Ohio to meet Rob Bell. I had read a couple of his books that profoundly affected my spiritual perspective. Even though I didn't agree with everything he said, I couldn't help admitting that he has a special gift to communicate and convey God's message in everyday language.

I took that trip by myself. I couldn't find anyone to go with me, and I didn't want to lose the opportunity to meet in person someone who had given me so much.

I arrived at a theater in Columbus on that cold night and I sat down to wait for the conference entitled, "Drops like Stars" by Rob Bell. The auditorium was more or less full. I would say there were about two thousand people there. Since I was alone, I was able to get a good seat in the fifth row.

In the middle of the conference, Rob asked a question that I considered trivial at the time. So trivial that I don't remember it exactly. But the question is not important; let's say that he asked something like, "Could everyone stand who has a vehicle?"

About eighty percent of the audience, I'd say, stood up. Rob asked us to look at each other. I looked around the auditorium and saw that almost everyone was standing up. Got it. Like I told you previously, I felt that the question didn't make a lot of sense; it seemed pretty irrelevant to me.

But Rob Bell wouldn't ask an irrelevant question, which I would confirm a few second later.

A few moments later, Rob asked this question: "Could all the people who have been affected by cancer, directly or indirectly, please stand up?"

In that moment, more than half of the audience stood up.

Rob asked us again to look at each other.

This time was different … profoundly different.

I lost my aunt and grandfather due to that monstrous illness. It also stole a close friend, Vanessa, who was taken from us much too young. When I think about cancer, I think about pain that touches my soul deeply.

That day, when I looked into the eyes of the other people around me, I was connected spiritually. It was as if I had known them a long time, as if they knew my pain, and I knew theirs.

Cancer had united us.

Pain unifies. It's a sad but also beautiful reality. Suffering connects us in a very deep way, in a way that success and prosperity never will.

That night Rob Bell said:

> Suffering connects us in a very deep way, in a way that success and prosperity never will.
> #innerherobook.com

Show me two parents with diametrically opposed political positions, with widely different beliefs about the most basic life issues, with very little in common, but each of them has a daughter that suffers from an eating disorder, and I will show you two parents who are united by a link that cuts across all those differences. Show me two mothers from different parts of the city with different environments, each one of them goes to jail to visit their son once a month, and I will show you two mothers who have a link that cuts across all those differences.[3]

In the movie *The Way* that I mentioned previously, there's a scene in which Tom, ready to start the pilgrimage, meets the chief of police who informed him of the death of his son. The chief speaks to Tom several times, but Tom doesn't pay attention. He is pretty distracted by his situation, but at one point, the captain says to Tom, "Mr. Avery, I also lost a son." The confession shakes Tom and brings him out of self-absorption, and for a second, there is a connection.

Donald Miller tells us, "Every conflict, no matter how difficult it may be, returns to bless the main character, if he faces his destiny with courage. Every conflict endured by human beings will bring a blessing."[4]

Connecting with others will be one of the greatest blessings that life will give you because those relationships will be the deepest and most long-lasting in your life.

4. Conflict helps you inspire others. John Maxwell says: "If you want to impress others, tell them about your successes; if you want to impact them, tell them about your failures."[5]

As I mentioned in the previous chapter, the story of your life will be as interesting and, may I add, inspiring, as the level of conflict that you are willing to overcome.

> Donald Miller tells us, "Every conflict, no matter how difficult it may be, returns to bless the main character, if he faces his destiny with courage. Every conflict endured by human beings will bring a blessing."
> #innerherobook.com

> The story of your life will be as interesting and, may I add, inspiring, as the level of conflict that you are willing to overcome.
> #innerherobook.com

Tony Melendez, after learning to play the guitar with his feet and making an appearance for the Pope, decided to devote his life to inspiring others. Why does listening to what Tony has to say inspire us? Because he went through conflict to get to where he is now. Do you want to inspire people? You need to be brave and take on conflict. And when you have come out on the other side, you will have a story to tell that will inspire many.

Dave Ramsey is a good example of this. Up to the present, he has built an empire based on personal financial education. Dave has become a millionaire twice. The first time, he lost it all.

After having become a millionaire in the real estate industry, Dave had to file bankruptcy at an early age. Based on the pain and suffering of that experience, he decided to devote his life to helping others get out of their financial straits and generate wealth.

To date, he has written several books that have made it to the *New York Times* bestseller list, a radio show broadcast across the entire US, and owns a company with more than four hundred employees in charge of sending his message to churches, nonprofit organizations, and companies.

But the most impressive thing about Dave is not the books he's sold, how successful his radio show is, or how big his company has grown. I had the chance to visit his company and learned of thousands of stories, written on each wall, of people whose lives were changed thanks to Dave.

What is the reason Dave has such an impact? Why is it when people listen to him they decide to change their lives and put their finances in order? Why would a family decide to eat rice and beans for two years in order to pay off their debts for a better future? Because Dave had walked the walk. He had been at the bottom and knew what it's like to be there. He understands what it's like to be destroyed, finished. When someone calls his show, drowning in desperation with creditors at their heels, Dave has been there. When somebody comes to him with excuses, he doesn't accept them, because he was once there too.

Dave Ramsey's conflict changed him into one of the most inspiring figures I've ever seen and someone who has changed more lives than most.

Imagine that one day you have the opportunity to meet a person who has been very successful in the area where you want to be successful. Let's say that you have been struggling for a couple of years to move your business forward, but you haven't been as successful as expected. You just approach him and ask, "Excuse me, if I could borrow a few minutes of your time, could you please tell me what you did to get to where you are right now?"

To which this recognized businessman replies, "To be honest, everything was very easy and fast. One day, I woke up with the desire to put this idea to work, and I did it. A few months later, I couldn't believe how successful I was. Every day, I pinch myself to make sure this is real."

Can you imagine an answer like that? Would it inspire you?

Imagine now that you are having some marriage problems and you decide to talk with a couple who has been married for fifty years and who has always impressed you with their love for one another.

You approach them, tell them about your problems, and ask them for advice. They reply: "We really don't understand why you are going through your situation. We must've been lucky because we've never fought. Everything has always been a bed of roses."

What about this answer? Could you learn anything from it? If on the other hand, this couple tells you about the difficult moments, about the conversation they had when they were considering separating, and the changes they made to save their marriage; or the businessman tells you about that dark night when he thought everything was lost; or when his partner whom he trusted defrauded him; or when he had to get up every morning for ten years, against all odds, to pursue what he has achieved. Wouldn't that be different? Wouldn't it be inspiring?

Your struggles, conflicts, obstacles, and problems will be an inspiration for others in the future. Conflict helps us to have a life inspiring to others. I see it as a virtuous cycle. Those who have come out of conflict inspire those who are just entering into it. Marriages that were once on the verge of divorce inspire couples going through problems; people who have overcome disease inspire those who have just been diagnosed; individuals who overcome bankruptcy inspire those who are in financial problems; and successful business men inspire those who are about to give up on their dream. This is the virtuous cycle of conflict and you can be part of it and make a difference.

The most supportive words that could ever offer to someone are: I know how you feel; I understand what you're going through. Elizabeth Kubler-Ross once said, "The most beautiful people I have met are those that have known defeat, suffering, struggle, loss and have found a way to get out of the depths. These people have appreciation, sensitivity and a comprehension about life that fills them with compassion, humility and a deep loving concern. Beautiful people don't emerge from nothing"[6]

5. Conflict prepares you for success. I have always been an avid lover of mountain sports. I feel that, in some way, when I am surrounded by nature, I connect with God and his creation. Since I enjoy the mountains, I have watched all the movies and television series related to the subject, especially if the mountain involved is Mount Everest.

Mount Everest is the highest mountain in the world at 29,029 feet above sea level. It is located along the border of China and Nepal. In fact, the border crosses directly through its summit.

Every year, hundreds of climbers try to reach the summit of this mountain, which has taken the lives of more than 140 people down throughout the years.

Like any expedition of this magnitude, it needs detailed planning, including the amount of time at each camp.

Mount Everest can't be climbed in just one leg. You have to spend time at multiple camps along the route to make sure that your body will manage the lack of oxygen and low pressure it has to face.

A curious fact I discovered a while ago is that people who want to climb Everest need to spend two weeks at Advanced Base Camp, located at twenty thousand feet above sea level.

That's two long weeks of headaches, sleepless nights, little appetite, constant vomiting, lack of energy, and boredom.

Why do they need to stay for two weeks? Because they are preparing their bodies to make the summit of Everest. They are going through an acclimatization process. Due to the lack of pressure at these altitudes because the amount of oxygen is much lower. The human body needs time to be able to increase its levels of red blood cells in the blood stream in order to carry the greatest amount of oxygen possible throughout the body.

Failure to acclimatize can be fatal. That is why it is infinitely preferable to put up with two horrible weeks of pain, fatigue, lack of appetite, vomiting, and extreme boredom in order to fulfill the dream of climbing to the top of the world.

Conflict prepares you for success; it prepares you for the summit of Mount Everest.

If you don't spend the two weeks at Advanced Base Camp, you will greatly decrease the likelihood of ever standing at the top of Mount Everest, beholding the most beautiful vista you could imagine, and returning home to tell about it.

One of the most common teachings in the world of mountain climbing is the following: going down the mountain after reaching the summit is even more dangerous than going up. More people die in the descent than the ascent.

I don't know if the fact that more people have died going down is true or not, but it makes sense.

> Conflict prepares you for success; it prepares you for the summit of Mount Everest. #innerherobook.com

The mountain climbers, in their passion to reach the peak use all their energy to get to it. Then, exhausted, they become careless in the descent, which sometimes leads to a fatal end.

Acclimating yourself correctly not only helps you to have energy and focus on the way to the top but also on the way down. The success of a mountain expedition is not only measured by whether or not you reach the peak, but by whether, after reaching the peak, you get home safe and sound.

Its the same with life. We're tired of hearing stories of folks who achieve success quickly only to see their lives destroyed shortly thereafter. Just turn on the TV and watch a show about Hollywood stars or famous singers. You will see story after story after story recounting failure, drugs, alcohol, etc.

Success changes people and it would be stupid to think that it wouldn't change you. I remember seeing a family a few years back who won a millionaire lottery, and when they received the check they said that the fortune wouldn't change who they were.

Everybody says the same thing, but almost everyone changes. You don't want your call, your passion, and your success to change your values and principles for the worse. That's why you need to acclimate yourself through conflict.

> You want to have sustained success, and the only way to get it is by building your character, keeping yourself humble, and never forgetting where you come from.
> #innerherobook.com

You want to have sustained success, and the only way to get it is by building your character, keeping yourself humble, and never forgetting where you come from. As I mentioned before, character is not built in a Jacuzzi in Hawaii but on the street, in the arena, in the battle. Every *no* that you get, every punch, every wound, failure—that is what is building who you really are. It is bringing out the real hero in you.

There is a story that goes after seeing the statue of the David by Michelangelo, the Pope asked, "How did you know what to remove from the stone?" to which Michelangelo replied, "Very simple, I just removed everything that didn't look like David".[7]

That is what conflict does in your life. It removes everything that doesn't look like you and brings the real hero inside of you into the light for all to see.

CHAPTER 11

CONFLICT AND WISDOM

IN 2013, I HAD THE OPPORTUNITY of meeting John Maxwell in person. John is one of the greatest experts on the subject of leadership that I've ever met. He's written more than seventy books, several of which have become *New York Times* bestsellers. In October 2013, I traveled to Mexico City to listen to him in person.

As one of those gifts from God and life, my friend Spencer Hoffman, the event organizer, gave me the opportunity to have some time with him during lunch hour.

More than fifteen years before, I'd read one of his books, followed by another, and another. At this point, I don't know exactly how many I've read, but there are many. What I mean is that meeting him in person was a big deal for me, and I was truly excited. Fifteen years earlier, I would never have imagined being face to face with the author of the book I was reading at that time. Often when we read a book, we feel the author is distant, unreachable, as if he inhabits an entirely different universe. But life sometimes surprises you, and that day, I was in for a real treat.

After lunch, in a more intimate atmosphere, he decided to respond to any questions the audience might have. After a few seconds of silence which highlighted our inabilities and fears in making a first step, someone got brave and asked the first question.

A few seconds after John responded, another question came forward, followed by another, then another.

I was deeply impressed by John's wisdom. It's one thing to write a book that can be edited a hundred times, seek advice on, or gather information from the Internet, and take you more than one year to write; or give a conference that you have months in advance to plan, rehearse, correct, and improve. It's one thing to write a book or give a conference, but it's another thing entirely to answer deep questions live.

Moments like these showcase a person's wisdom. And John Maxwell impressed me. I got the impression he could write a book every answer he gave, that he had files full of years of information and wisdom in his mind, and in a matter of mere seconds, he could find the correct file, attach it to the correct story, and explain it using just the right words to communicate his point in the most effective way possible. It wasn't only the information he had, but the pauses, the highs and lows of his voice, his body language. It was everything.

It was wisdom in its most perfect expression.

The interesting thing about it is when I had the opportunity to listen to John that day, both at lunch and in the three plenary sessions he delivered, he only spoke about failure, suffering, and conflict. He told us about his initial struggles as a writer, his early failures as a speaker, and the seven different times he changed jobs in which each one he made less than the previous.

Every conflict, every failure, every second of suffering had imparted him wisdom.

There is a natural process of growth in attaining wisdom for human beings for every activity in

> There is a journey, a process that you have to go through to attain the wisdom and mastery of whatever you are passionate about.
> #innerherobook.com

which he wishes to be successful. Regardless of whether your call to adventure is to become a musician, painter, or businessman, or move to Africa to dedicate your life to providing clean water to those who need a drink, there is a journey, a process that you have to go through to attain the wisdom and mastery of whatever you are passionate about.

And everything starts after you accept the call to adventure. After the initiating incident plunges you into the story. In that moment, we are all profoundly happy. We have decided to start living the life that we once dreamed of. We finally enroll in that literary course or singing contest. We kneel down before the love of our life. We throw the last cigarette in the trash, or end that abusive relationship that only brought us suffering and tears. At that moment, you enter a phase in which you are "unconsciously incompetent," which is followed by other stages.

1. Unconsciously Incompetent. In this first stage you are incompetent, but you don't know it yet. That is why you are filled with hope and motivation.

The day I was hired for my first job, I celebrated. When I was transferred to the US, I celebrated. When I signed the contract to publish this book, I went out and celebrated. There is something natural and positive in celebrations. As human beings we like to celebrate before commencing a story. But what it really shows is ignorance about the impending conflict. In a movie, you never see Frodo celebrating because he now has to battle giants and armies in order to destroy the ring. And, you never see Rocky celebrating because he finally gets to fight against the Russian giant, Drago. Heroes in stories understand that they are about to face a trial that they are not prepared for and probably never will be.

Nevertheless, we celebrate.

I have nothing against celebrating little victories, especially if they lead us into a better story. The problem is that what we're celebrating is not the beginning of the adventure, but the culmination of it. We think that the contract for the book that we signed, the promotion we got, that new client that we gained we got because we have the ability to handle it. But it's the contrary. We got them because we do not yet have the ability, and we need to grow through that new adventure.

The stage where you are unconsciously incompetent is also called the honeymoon phase, and it is worth noting that you will be successful. At least for a while.

It is called the honeymoon because it resembles those first months of marriage that we experience. If you've been married, you know what I am talking about. Everything is beautiful and perfect. The trip, the moon, the food, the intimacy. We don't get annoyed by anything. We get home from work early to be with our loved one, we are flexible, and we think about each other constantly.

That stage is based on enthusiasm. As a new husband or wife, you satisfy your partner deeply by your enthusiasm. As a sales person or new businessman, you influence your clients with your enthusiasm. As a new musician or athlete, you make important progress by means of your enthusiasm.

But little frustrations and failures naturally begin to appear. You no longer enjoy your husband leaving his underwear on the bathroom floor, and you have a spat; or a small pain in your leg keeps you from running your goal for the day; or one of your prospects is no longer answering the phone and sends you a text message saying he will not buy as agreed; or your blog is not receiving the visitors that you were expecting; or it turns out that learning to play the piano is not that easy.

Those are little failures that begin to extinguish your excitement. And since this stage is based solely on enthusiasm, when it suffers a decline, so does everything else.

The reality is that during this phase, you were always incompetent; your incompetence level never changed. It's simply the first time that you realized it, that you looked yourself in the mirror and accepted the fact that you don't know what you' doing.

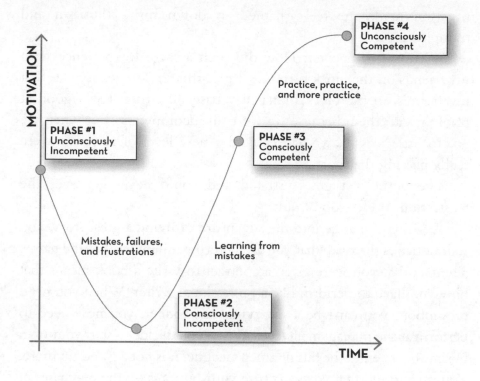

2. Consciously Incompetent. "We are incompatible!" many people say, referring to their spouse, when they get to this phase. Statements like *I'm no good at sales*, or *I don't have a musical ear*, or *I wasn't born to be a businessman*, or *that whole idea of launching a blog was a mistake*, or *building a business was easier in the past.* These thoughts flood the individual in this phase.

I remember when I decided to be part of a baseball team. I was about twelve or thirteen years old. I don't really remember, but I do recall perfectly the happiness I felt that Friday going with my father to get my shoes, ball, and baseball glove.

I played baseball all day long with my friends on the block that weekend. I always identified with Jose Canseco, and I liked to imagine that I was him. I was happy, feeling that I had been born for baseball. I was unconsciously incompetent.

My journey through baseball didn't last long, probably a couple of months maximum. From the first day, things went badly for me. I was playing right fielder when I got hit in the head by a ball. This situation made me feel ashamed; it down my enthusiasm and trampled on it.

What had happened? How did such a special experience with my friends on the block turn into a nightmare? The reality was that my friends on the block didn't play baseball either. I was good at playing with them because we were all incompetent. But when we got to little league, we had entered a new level of play. We were really playing the sport.

The point is I got frustrated and could never get over the frustration. Pretty soon I quit.

When you plunge into the adventure of living a great story, you will notice right away that you are entering a new level of the game. The fact that you were given a contract to write a book means that now you have to perform like a professional writer. When you get a promotion, you can't be a supervisor any longer; you now need to perform at the management level. When you decide to start your own business, you enter the businessmen's league. It is not a game anymore. You understand that you can't base your business on the purchases of your mom and your friends. You are in a different league.

This is the point where most people give up.

There are three mistakes we make during this phase that destroy the possibility of following our call.

The first mistake is we are not aware this stage exists and that we are going through it. We take the results personally. Thus, we say things like, *We are not compatible,* or *I don't have a musical ear,* or *I am not good at sales.* We take the outcome personally, as if somehow God had said, I am going to give you the dream of becoming a great businessman but will take away the strength needed to make it, or I am going to give you passion for music but will take away your musical ear. I don't know. I am not going to speak for God, but that never made sense to me.

The world is full of incompetents, people who in the eyes of the world did not have what it takes to do this or that, and then somehow broke all the rules and molds. One of them is Erik, whom I got to know a few years back.

The day I met him, I sat half-bored at a work conference, but an hour or so before it ended, they announced that Erik Weihenmayer was coming to meet us and tell us a little of his story. We were told that Erik was a climber, which immediately got my attention as you might imagine. Then, we were told that Erik had climbed the highest mountains in the world including Aconcagua, Mount McKinley, and Mount Everest. Okay, now they really had my attention.

A few second later, Erik showed up. He was blind.

He was born with a rare disease that left him blind when he was thirteen. He said after that, he could no longer play with a ball, but when he was taken to a small rocky hill, he discovered that his hands could be his eyes, and he climbed it. That event opened Erik up to a world of infinite possibilities that brought him to climb Mount McKinley in 1995, to carry the Olympic Torch in 1996, to climb Mount Kilimanjaro in 1997, Aconcagua in 1999, and Mount Everest in 2001.

On one of his frequent expeditions, he met a group of blind children in Tibet who were living in a sort of orphanage because their lack of sight was considered a curse and had been rejected by their parents, family members, and the community. In 2004, Erik took these children on a hike in the Himalayas to show them what they were capable of in spite of their disability.

The day I met him, he made the following comment to us:

The world writes off so many things as impossible very quickly, simply because we haven't found the systems to cope with the challenge in a non-conventional way.

I believe that there is a blurred line between the things that we can do and the things that we can't. There is nothing more exciting than being a pioneer. Go through those lines and overthrow those obstacles that are normally conceived in our minds.

There was a moment when I felt that I had the necessary skills and qualifications to climb Mount Everest. Many people laughed; but some of them believed and that was all that was needed.

Sometimes you have to take others' expectations, throw them in the trash and reach your maximum potential.[1]

If Erik can climb Mount Everest being blind and Tony Melendez can play the guitar with no arms before thousands of people including the Pope, then you can do whatever you want. You weren't born without a musical ear, or without the skill to be a good salesman, or incompatible with your spouse, or bad at baseball. You simply have to learn to do it well. That is the greatest mistake I have seen. Do not take it personally, it is a natural and necessary phase in the development of your story. It will come and it will go, and you will come out victorious on the other side.

The second mistake we make during this phase is we compare ourselves with others, especially individuals who have already gone through this phase. This brings great frustration and demotivation. When I think back on it, I can see how a big part of my frustration on the baseball team came from the comparison of how well they played against how poorly I did. But the fact is they had been playing together for months, maybe years. It was a natural growth process that I needed to go through, but unfair comparisons led me to give it all up.

Once, a person approached John Maxwell and told him:

"Now I know what I want to do with my life." "Really? And what do you want to do with your life?"

Maxwell asks.

"I want to do what you do. I was looking around the room and there are about two thousand people. I know how much I paid for my ticket, so that gives me an idea of how much you make for each of these conferences. I have seen how people buy your books outside the theatre. That is what I want to do."

John laughs and says:

"Ok. So you want to do what I do," he paused; "The question isn't whether you want to do what I do, but: are you willing to do what I did?"[2]

The fact that John fills a theater with two thousand, five thousand, or forty thousand people is not due to the work that he does today. It's because of the work that he's done for more than thirty years. The reason his latest book is on the bestsellers list is not necessarily because of its content or the marketing, but because of the more than seventy books that he's published in the past.

Nevertheless, we want to start a career as a writer and we compare ourselves with John, when in the first chapter we can't even write more than two pages.

Don't compare yourself with others. That won't help you or anybody else. Remember that you are living your story. It is yours and it is personal. The struggle is with yourself, with resistance, and nothing more.

The third mistake we make in this phase is making important or drastic decisions while we are going through it.

> Don't compare yourself with others. That won't help you or anybody else. Remember that you are living your story.
> #innerherobook.com

Life has a way of twisting fate in a comical way.. When I finished university, Juan Carlos, one of my best friends, and I took different paths. I started working for Procter & Gamble while Juan Carlos started working for the equally well-known firm Gillette.

A couple of years later, Procter & Gamble purchased Gillette and the employees of that company moved to the building where I worked. After the reorganization, Juan Carlos became the Financial Manager of the Department where I was working. In fact, our desks were less than ten feet apart from each other.

As with every transition, there were trying moments for the Gillette employees. I remember talking to Juan Carlos when he was going through one of those difficult moments of the transition.

That day Juan Carlos gave me a lesson that I will never forget.

"Sometimes we're up and sometimes we're down," he said as he drew an imaginary curve with his finger.

"I learned that I never make drastic decisions if I am in the lowest part of the curve. Ever. I never run from something, I run toward it."

> If you are going to make a change, don't do it to escape something, do it running toward something better.
> #innerherobook.com

And that's what he did. Over time, he resigned. But he didn't do it trying to run away because things were hard. Rather, he did it when he had already overcome the hard circumstances and things were going well. If you are going to make a change, don't do it to escape something, do it running toward something better.

Trust in what I am going to tell you. This phase will pass. Little by little, you will learn the skills, techniques, and attitudes you need to grow in the field where your passion lies. There are no shortcuts, you need to go through it.

And all of a sudden, in the middle of frustration, you will start practicing the piano again, and without expecting it yourself, melody will surface. You will pick up the phone once again in the middle of discouragement, and, magically, some person will tell you yes. You will put on your running shoes, and, at least for a little while, you will feel happy. You will begin to experience little victories. At first, many failures and only a few victories. In time, a few failures are coupled with a few victories. And, then, the time will come when the victories will start to overtake the failures. You will start being consciously competent.

3. Consciously Competent. During this phase you already know what's needed to be successful. You have learned that when you do things in a certain way, you turn the results in your favor. In this phase, you have to be focused, detail-oriented, and execute everything in a well-thought-out manner.

The good thing about this phase is that many things are turning out well. You have learned how to do them, but you need a great deal of energy and focus for them to turn out the way you want.

When I ran my first half marathon, I didn't enjoy the scenery, the weather, or the festivities around the race. I needed to be focused. I had never run such a distance before, so all my energy was focused on my performance in the race. My only goal was to finish.

I was focused on the map, my watch, my water, and my heartbeat. I knew that if I followed a pattern, I should get to the end successfully.

This phase is like playing a piece of music you've worked on so much with your guitar, but your mind is focused on its execution—its rhythm, chords, hands, etc. You played the song but didn't really enjoy it. It's like when you learned to drive a car for the first time. Your mind was full of information and processes—traffic signals, the steering wheel, the gas pedal, brakes, and in some cases, the song on the radio.

Surely, you have seen in a movie or even in real life well-trained martial arts students endlessly practicing the same kick or punch, over and over.

These students have gone through a process in which they have been taught the technique and they have learned it. The trainer looks for the punch and kick to come without thinking, for it to move from the conscious to the unconscious.

The only way to move from one phase to the next is through practice. Just as I ran my half marathon focused on the map and my heartbeat, there were other people who were running and enjoying the view, the people around them, and the moment.

In the previous phase (consciously incompetent) the most important thing was to keep at it and learn from your errors. Practice and more practice is the most critical thing about this phase. Constant practice over time will move the knowledge you acquired in a conscious state, where you need to be focused and thinking, to an unconscious state, where you do it naturally.

How can John Maxwell open up the floor for questions from the audience and in every answer deliver a profound and effective message? Because practice (speaking at thousands of conferences and writing more than seventy books) moved his knowledge from a conscious state to the unconscious state.

4. Unconsciously Competent. This is the wisdom stage. Your passion, experiences, learning, failures, and successes have been internalized in an unconscious way. You don't need to think in order to react any more. Now you can play that piece on your piano and enjoy it, run the marathon and think about something else. Now you know how to do what has to be done, and you do it well automatically.

Do you remember when you learned how to ride a bike? You got so excited when it was given to you. You saw your neighbors riding full speed through the neighborhood and wanted to go out to ride it immediately (unconsciously incompetent). Finally, mom or dad put your helmet on you and went out with you to live that experience, which for some reason is magical for all of us.

When you started riding your bike, you realized that keeping your balance was not an easy task, that falls hurt and pedaling was tiring (consciously incompetent).

I am sure that at some point you wanted to give up, cried, stomped your feet and got upset. What had looked so beautiful and desirable, all of a sudden, had turned into a nightmare—skinned knees, tears, fear, and lack of confidence.

But later, out of the blue–for a brief period of time–almost magically and inexplicably, you sensed that you were keeping your balance for the first time. You tried again several times and it happened again. You didn't fall all the time; you were mastering your bike more and more each time.

Afterwards, you could ride your bike a few feet, possibly no more than a ride around the block. If you could have seen your face, you were so concentrated on not falling that instead of enjoyment, it seemed like a penance (consciously competent).

Little by little, with practice, you stopped thinking about balance, brakes, and pedals. Everything started to flow automatically (unconsciously competent) and you could start focusing on the scenery and enjoy the wind in your hair when you were speeding.

Everything that had been a challenge weeks before was no longer. Conflict launches you into a process toward achieving wisdom. Regardless of whether your call is to learn how to play a musical instrument, become a successful businessman, start a blog, become a Hollywood actor, or embark on a sailboat to travel around the world, you need to go through these four stages to attain wisdom.

> Conflict launches you into a process toward achieving wisdom.
> #innerherobook.com

One day in 2011, while changing channels, I saw Erik Weihenmayer again, the blind guy that climbed Mount Everest. On this occasion, he was competing on a televison show called *Expedition Impossible*. In this competition, the participants have to run, climb, hurl themselves over waterfalls, swim, pedal, and row, among other things. The competitors were firemen, military men, police officers, and other athletes that would beat me in any physical activity if I dared to challenge them.

Erik got second place. A blind man had won against more than ten of the best athletes in the world. Even though he didn't get first place, he felt like he did.

Malcolm Gladwell, in his fascinating book *Outliers*, deciphers a common factor among some of the most successful people that you can think of. He studied the lives of Bill Gates, Steve Jobs, The Beatles, even Mozart. The amazing revelation that comes from his findings is that more than talent or opportunity, the real reason for these people's massive success was practice.

He defines it as The 10,000 Hour Rule. He indicates that to become a world-class expert, you need ten thousand hours of practice to make it.

In his book, he discusses the results of a study that a psychologist named Anders Ericsson made in 1990 to determine the reason for success among musicians.

He compared professional musicians with amateurs. About the results, he writes:

> The most striking thing about Ericsson's study is that he and his colleagues couldn't find any pianist with "natural talent," musicians who could effortlessly get to the top by only practicing a fraction of what their colleagues practiced. Neither could they find "unlucky pianists," people who worked as hard as anyone else, but simply didn't have what it took to get to the top. Their research indicates that once the musician has enough skill to get into music school, the only difference between one pianist and another is how hard he or she practices. That's it. And something else, the people who were at the top of the top not only worked harder than the rest. They work much, much, much harder.[3]

Neurologist Daniel Levitin, in his book *This is your Brain on Music: The Science of Human Obsession*, explains:

> The conclusions of multiple studies always end up saying that ten thousand hours of practice are necessary to reach the level of world-class expertise in any field. In study after study of composers, basketball players, fiction writers, ice skaters, pianists, chess players, criminal geniuses, etc., this number shows up again and again…. Apparently, it takes the brain that long to reach the level necessary for real mastery.[4]

When Bill Gates founded Microsoft, he had already programmed more than ten thousand hours. When Mozart composed the first symphony that was considered a masterpiece, he had practiced more than ten thousand hours. When The Beatles began to become famous, they had already practiced more than ten thousand hours.

Practice, practice, practice will make the difference. Practice will make you unconsciously competent, and when you get to that point, the entire world will be on your side.

CHAPTER 12

CONFLICT AND FAILURE

IN THE SCENE of the movie *The Hobbit* that I mentioned previously, Bilbo asks Gandalf whether he can promise that Bilbo will come back, to which Gandalf replies. "No, but if you do, you will never be the same.

On various occasions, different people have asked me a similar question. After enthusiastically telling me about their plans and dreams, about the new adventure they want to undertake, they ask me something like, *If I do everything we have talked about, can you guarantee that I will be successful? If I decide to pursue my dream, can you assure me that I'll find it at the end of the road?*

I believe that the real question they want to ask me is something like this, *Do you think I might fail?* This leaves me with an easy answer. Yes, of course.

The reality is that nothing guarantees that we are going to be

> The question is not whether you are going to fail or not, but how you are going to react when you fail.
>
> #innerherobook.com

as successful as we imagined. There is fear, there is resistance, and, of course, there are the plans of God.

The question is not whether you are going to fail or not, but how you are going to react when you fail. There is no success without failure. Nobody is successful all the time. Success is always an uphill battle.

Every hero fails. Rocky loses; Bilbo nearly gets everyone killed; Maximus is imprisoned and sold as a slave while his whole family is killed; Rudy fails several times trying to get into university. In those moments we will either let failure define us or prepare us.

By studying failure, I have reached the following conclusions.

1. **Failure is not the same as being a failure.** Something I often observe in people who are going through conflict is that they confuse the word failure with being a failure, which is clearly not the same.

> The fact that you've gone through failure doesn't make you a failure. #innerherobook.com

I remember my greatest failures like they were yesterday. These events affected the deepest part of my identity and made me feel like I was a failure. The reality is that failure is an event, not a person, and we need to make that distinction. We need to separate the event from the person. The fact that you've gone through failure doesn't make you a failure.

Michael Jordan is one of the best basketball players in history and one of the best athletes in the world. Among his achievements is having taken his team, The Chicago Bulls, to six NBA championships. Five times he has been named MVP of the professional league. His triumphs make a long list that will be hard to match in the future.

In 1994, Michael Jordan wrote a short book called *I Can't Accept not Trying* where he stated, "I have lost three hundred games, have missed more than nine thousand shots, twenty six times my team counted on me to score the winning basket and I missed".[1]

Michael Jordan failed hundreds of times. Nevertheless, he is remembered not as one of the best, but the best basketball player in history. Failure is an event, not a person.

Don't let failure define you as a failure, because you are not. You failed in the past and will fail in the future. But you will always be the hero of your story.

> You failed in the past and will fail in the future. But you will always be the hero of your story.
> #innerherobook.com

2. Don't be afraid to fail, be afraid to fail twice doing the same thing. Like I said before, failure is an event, a fact, not a person. A person who is a failure is one who, when he or she fails, makes excuses their ally. The person who is a failure will always say that the economy, the new laws, my wife, my husband, my children, etc., are the reasons for their failures. Consequently, the loser doesn't learn and makes the same mistake again.

My first years with Procter & Gamble, I was trained in a continuous improvement process well known in industry called why-why analysis. The process is used every time we have a malfunction of any kind of importance for the organization. This process is very simple. After detecting the malfunction, we wrote down the reasons why that malfunction happened. After that, we went through the same process with each one of the reasons. We wrote down why those reasons had happened and so on.

> A person who is a failure is one who, when he or she fails, makes excuses their ally.
> #innerherobook.com

This process guided us to create a branching tree of reasons of why the malfunction had taken place and get to a root cause to be able to correct it. A hypothetical example might be:

"We had to stop the production lines in our plant."

"Why? Because all the inventories of raw material X ran out."

"Why? Because we didn't order the amount that we needed."

"Why? Because there is a significant difference between the forecast demand and the customer orders that we get."

"Why? Because we didn't consider in our demand a special event that customer X was going to put on."

"Why? Because the information was never communicated from the sales department to the planning department."

"Why? Because we do not have an established process through which the sales department informs the planning department about special events."

When we got to this point, it was simple to determine that a monthly meeting between the planning manager and the sales manager was needed to go over our customers' special events which would permanently solve the problem.

This process helps the company avoid using band aid solutions like "order more raw material X," and creates permanent solutions that keep them from making the same mistakes.

> Remember, don't be afraid of failure. Be afraid to fail twice doing the same thing.
> #innerherobook.com

When we fail, we need to do our own why-why analysis. Only then can we get to the root, to the real cause of the failure, learn from it, and move forward in the right direction. Ask yourself why you failed and don't settle for a superficial reason. Ask yourself why again and again and again until you get to the root cause of the failure. In that moment, you will be able to truly learn and correct the problem for good.

Remember, don't be afraid of failure. Be afraid to fail twice doing the same thing.

3. Admit failure promptly. The moment you fail at something, the sooner you admit it, the better. You need to admit it to yourself first and then to any others affected by it. Never become a victim of the situation.

Becoming a victim of your situations, hard knocks, obstacles, and failures doesn't do anything but sink you deeper and deeper. It could be that momentarily you feel satisfied by the attention, love and pity of others, but you are receiving that temporary satisfaction at a very high price. A price that isn't worth paying.

On this subject, Steven Pressfield says that passive-aggressive behavior becomes apparent when we insist on being the victim. When we choose to remain the victim, we generally use direct or indirect threats to manipulate others in order to get gratification. It is gratification obtained with honest effort or a worthwhile contribution of our love, dedication, experience, or other effort. This kind of victim controls other people with threats of misery if they don't comply with his/her demands. This victim uses their illness or mental condition to make others come to their rescue, and then make them hostages of the unhealthy condition of the alleged victim.[2]

Becoming a victim is exactly the opposite of responding to your call. If you are doing so, stop it.

No matter how much you are thinking that the reasons of your failure were external, there is always something that was your responsibility. Assume that responsibility. Don't make yourself a victim, admit your mistakes, learn and move forward.

4. Understand that life is made for second chances. Back in 2013, I had the wonderful opportunity of meeting Diana Nyad. Diana was the first and only person to date who has been able to swim from Cuba to the coast of Miami. The distance covers a total of 110 miles.

The journey is nearly impossible. You have to swim for more than

> No matter how much you are thinking that the reasons of your failure were external, there is always something that was your responsibility. #innerherobook.com

sixty hours, day and night, through an ocean full of dangers, including the most dangerous types of jellyfish and aggressive sharks.

In 1978, at twenty eight years old, Diana traveled to Cuba to attempt her adventure. After swimming forty-two hours, her team was forced to get her out of the water because the raging waves were making her crash against a cage they had built to protect her from sharks.

After this failure, Diana didn't swim for more than thirty years. Let me repeat this. She didn't swim for more than thirty years.

When Diana was sixty-two, her mother passed away at the age of eighty-two years old. Her mom's death made Diana reflect upon her life. Assuming that she would get to live a similar age, she concluded that she had more or less twenty-two years left.

The day when Diana told us her story, she said, "When I turned sixty and thought about the years of life I had left, I decided that the best way to get the best value out of the twenty- two years I had left was to participate fully, to be completely alive, alert, and awake every minute of every day. It was to take part in the now so fully as not to leave any time to regret the past."

That new way of thinking led her to receive a new call to adventure. She said it came to her all of a sudden. a desire to try once again for the dream she had put at the back of her mind thirty years earlier. Three decades later, without having swum since, she was going to attempt to swim from Cuba to Florida.

When asked about her motivation to attempt the journey again, she said, "Because I want to prove to other sixty-year-old people that it is never too late to start living your dreams."

On August 7, 2011, thirty-three years after the last attempt, Diana dove into the ocean off the coast of Cuba to finally make her dream a reality.

Twenty-nine hours later, due to powerful currents, a pain in her shoulder, and the beginning of an asthma attack, Diana was forced to abandon her attempt at her dream.

On September 23, 2011, Diana tried again, only to give up forty hours later due to a severe jellyfish attack that affected her respiratory system and required her to abandon the journey.

On August 18, 2012, one year later, Diana made her fourth attempt to get from Cuba to the US shores when again a jellyfish attack prevented her from fulfilling her dream.

On August 31, 2013, Diana started her final attempt at being the first person to swim the route between Cuba and Florida. Fifty-three hours later, on September 2nd at 1:55 p.m., Diana finally reached the shore of Key West, Florida.

When she got out of the water, among hundreds of fans and reporters, she said to the world, "I got three messages. One, we should never, ever give up. Two, you are never too old to chase your dreams. Three, it looks like a solitary sport, but it's a team".[3]

Life gave Diana Nyad a second, third, fourth, and fifth chance. Life has a second chance for you. That is what life is made of, second chances.

Life's beauty is found more in the struggle than the victory. Conflict, the falls, hard knocks, and failures are the best weapons that you have to bring out the diamond inside of you. In the same way that gold is purified through fire, who you become at the end of the process is the best gift you can receive.

One of the most profound and true sayings that has always inspired me was written by Theodore Roosevelt. It's called "The Man in the Arena," and it goes like this:

> Life has a second chance for you. That is what life is made of, second chances.
> #innerherobook.com

It is not the critic who counts; not the man who points out how the strong man stumbles, or where the doer of deeds could have done them better. The credit belongs to the man who is actually in the arena, whose face is marred by dust and sweat and blood; who strives valiantly; who errs, who comes short again and again, because there is no effort without error and shortcoming; but who does actually strive to do the deeds; who knows great enthusiasms, the great devotions; who spends himself in a worthy cause; who at the best knows in the end the triumph of high achievement, and who at the worst, if he fails, at least fails while daring greatly, so that his place shall never be with those cold and timid souls who neither know victory nor defeat.[4]

Roosevelt illustrates perfectly what a hero is. He's the one who, with his face marred by dust and sweat and blood, strives valiantly. Every hero needs to go through the most critical point of the conflict. A crossroads where he needs to make a decision: he either decides to draw strength where he doesn't have any, or he gives up to get the immediate relief of going back to the ordinary world. Every hero needs to go through the resurrection process.

PART FOUR

RESURRECTION

CHAPTER 13

RESURRECTION

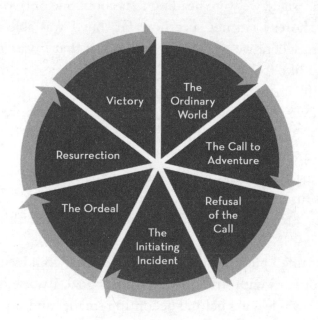

AFTER MORE THAN FIVE YEARS without visiting my home country, I was able to return. In spite of all of its problems, she felt like it was mine. Or, better said, I felt like I was part of her. To be able to see my family members and friends was worth it all. When you have been out of your country for so long, to be able to go back gives you a sense of belonging. It's like the story of the prodigal son that goes back home, and his father welcomes him with open arms. That is the way I was welcomed by Venezuela.

As part of the trip, we went to Morrocoy National Park, one of the most beautiful areas of Venezuela. This place is full of white-sandy beaches, untouched islands, and crystal-clear waters. A real gift of nature.

We went to visit my aunt, my father's sister who years ago had decided to flee the insanity of crowded cities and move to this place. The paradise that thousands of people enjoy only a few days of the year became her constant reality.

One morning, when we were ready to board a motor boat that would take us to one of the islands, my aunt proposed we go by kayak. The island we were heading to is about one or two kilometers from the shore, I am not sure how far, but I was able to see that island from where we were. Despite the fact that I wasn't as trained as I would like to have been, it didn't look to be so difficult, and I accepted the challenge to adventure.

When we reached the shore and said good-bye to the rest of the family who was going to travel happily in the motor boat, I got in the kayak and started to row hard.

The first few meters were a bit difficult because I had to battle the waves that, very similar to resistance, wanted to push me back to the shore. After I passed those initial waves, everything became easier.

Every time I put the paddle into the water, I could feel my kayak moving forward with strength toward my goal. I was excited to see the shore I was leaving behind becoming smaller and smaller. There was a virtuous cycle of results and motivation. Every time I rowed, I could feel my progress, and looking behind me, the sea shore was increasingly distant. The island that I was heading to was clearer and bigger compared to the way it looked before.

Everything was going marvelously when suddenly I realized that something was changing. The seashore I was leaving behind was no longer shrinking, and the island that I was heading toward wasn't getting any bigger. No matter how hard I was rowing, I felt that I was in the same spot. There was no progress, and my arms started to give out.

When you embark on an adventure, be it rowing to a distant island or starting a major project or business venture, it is normal to believe that you are going to make it through quickly.

We start projects, dreaming that we are going to change the world. We start a business with the conviction that we are going to be financially free. We start a diet or exercise plan decided we're improving our health permanently.

But all of us get to this point in which, no matter how hard we row, the sea shore that we left behind doesn't shrink, and the island we are heading to no longer gets bigger. We row and row, but nothing happens. Customers hide and don't return the phone calls. Those who promised to help have run away. The scale shows weight loss has stopped. And, our bills keep accumulating.

In that moment, we get frustrated and quit. We decide to change to a different story, a simpler adventure.

There is a term commonly used by runners, especially marathon runners, known as "the wall." It is something that happens to the body around mile eighteen of the marathon. Runners feel extreme fatigue and a loss of energy. Some athletes say that it feels as if someone put forty-pound weights on each leg. Each step is hell.

The cause is due to a decrease of glucose in the muscles and liver. This causes a deep heaviness in the legs, pain, muscular fatigue, and can even cause a certain level of clinical depression.

Hitting the wall is the most difficult moment in a marathon. It's not uncommon to see runners at that stage begin to walk instead of run, fall or faint, even sit down and cry.

This is the time when many give up.

There is also another common term in the sports world called a "second wind." Even if the reasons for a second wind are still not fully understood, testimonials of several athletes point out that it is like a new wave of energy wave that your body receives almost miraculously and sends a charge through you carrying you to the finish line.

A second wind carries runners to the finish line.

Not everyone experiences a second wind. What has been scientifically proven is that those who don't experience it are the ones who have given up.

A second wind is God's gift to those who are persistent, to those who make up their minds to take one more step, who keep rowing even though the island isn't getting bigger, those who continue selling, practicing, exercising, and praying. It is for them the magical moment when light emerges from the darkness, and what was impossible becomes true.

> And then I remembered that a story is not a story without an ending. #innerherobook.com

And so, that day, in the middle of the ocean, tired and frustrated, I kept rowing. No matter how hard I rowed though, nothing happened. I got trapped in the middle of the problem. Neither logic nor the laws of physics seemed to work for me. I just stopped for a second; I needed to catch my breath. And then I remembered that a story is not a story without an ending. If a boat was sent out to find me there would be no story, and I had to protect the story. If I didn't make it through, there would be no story for this book, and my children and my grandchildren would never have a chance to hear about it. So I decided to believe and kept rowing and rowing, and rowing.

And, as Donald Miller said, "You keep rowing even if you've lost all your strength, even if you don't make any progress. Out of the blue, all of a sudden, the shore of the island starts growing and growing fast. Palm trees are bigger now and you can see the rocks in detail and the shore comes to you and welcomes you home".[1]

That second wind is what is known in the world of stories as "Resurrection."

Resurrection is a point of life or death for your dream. Christoper Vogler says, "Darkness and death merge in a last and desperate effort that precedes their final defeat. It is a sort of final exam for the hero who will have to pass once again to demonstrate the learned lessons in the course of the odyssey. These moments of death and resurrection transform the hero."[2]

> Resurrection is a point of life or death for your dream.
> #innerherobook.com

In good movies, you can clearly recognize this resurrection moment in the life of the hero. Luke Skywalker in *Star Wars* is apparently dead, but miraculously survives. Frodo in *The Lord of the Rings* is unconscious on a rock when he unexpectedly gets up and accomplishes his goal. Brad Pitt as death itself in *Meet Joe Black*, decides at the last minute to restore life to the movie's protagonist so the love story can be completed. Even in movies like *Gladiator*, the death of Maximus brings the desired reform in Rome that Marcus Aurelius wants.

If you think for a minute about people who have impacted the world in a significant way, you will realize that they had to go through a resurrection process. Dave Ramsey filed bankruptcy, Steve Jobs was fired from the company that he himself founded. Nelson Mandela was imprisoned for decades for no other crime than challenging the evil in this world.

However, the list of those who fought and experienced resurrection is a thousand times smaller than the list of those who gave up. The sad reality is that most people just give up.

One of the saddest yet most beautiful stories I have heard is that of John Kennedy Toole. John was born in 1937 in New Orleans in a middle class family. From the time he was little, he had a passion for the arts, but especially writing. Shortly after graduating from university, Toole started to write a novel called *A Confederacy of Dunces* that was rejected many times by publishers of its time.

Suffering from depression as a result of the failure of his dream, Toole committed suicide by connecting a hose to the exhaust pipe of his vehicle and running it in through the window of the car. Toole died when he was thirty-one.

That day, in Biloxi, Mississippi, Toole not only gave up on his dream, but on his own life.

But the story didn't end there.

After his suicide, Toole's mother decided to publish the work to prove to the world his son's talent. For a period of five years she sent the manuscript to seven publishers only to have it rejected again and again. She used to say that every time she got a rejection, something in her would slowly die.

She finally got in touch with the novelist Walker Percy and asked him to read the literary work. Percy liked it and was able to get the work printed for the first time.

After its launch in 1980, the novel attracted the literary world, and a year later John Kennedy Toole posthumously won the Pulitzer Prize in Literature.

A Confederacy of Dunces has been translated into eighteen languages and sold more than a million and a half copies worldwide. John Kennedy Toole gave up too soon. In his darkest hour, he gave up in the middle of the ordeal. Toole confused failing with being a failure. Toole didn't understand that suffering, failure, and conflict are part of a phase that one has to overcome. Toole decided not to row any more.

One the other hand, Toole's mother persevered, motivated perhaps by the most powerful feeling ever felt, the love of a parent for a child. She fought because she believed in her son's talent, she held on to the belief within her that eventually the world would be ready for her son's novel. The mere possibility of the publication of the work, perhaps, became the only way to resurrect a part of him and offer it to the world. The point here is that she didn't give up until she saw her desire become a reality. The mother resurrected her son, and the son's work resurrected his mother.

In the end, a story was created. A story worth telling. The tragic and possibly cowardly suicide of Toole left the story incomplete.

And incomplete stories simply die as time goes on. Toole's mother finished the story; she brought it to completion. And out of that came a Pulitzer, more than one million copies sold, and a story that has been included as part of this book, which I am sure has impacted you.

Don't leave your story incomplete. It doesn't matter if it's as small and meaningless as a ride in a kayak or as grand and important as a literary work worthy of a Pulitzer. Incomplete stories are forgotten. Never leave your story incomplete.

The same way that the literal resurrection of Jesus changed the course of history and impacted millions of people, the resurrection process that you need to go through will not only be important for you but for many others around you.

> Incomplete stories are forgotten. Never leave your story incomplete.
> #innerherobook.com

That was the case of Betty Waters' story, a story of love and devotion like few others. A story of resurrection.

In 1983, Kenny Waters, Betty's brother, was sentenced to life in prison for the alleged murder of Katharina Brow, a horrible crime that had been perpetrated three years earlier in Massachusetts.

Kenny and Betty had always been very close. Despite his imprisonment, they would chat every week. Then, Betty, concerned because she hasn't receive Kenny's phone calls, hears that Kenny has tried to kill himself (initiating incident).

When Betty is finally able to talk to her brother, he says to her that he can't stand to live his life in prison for something he didn't do. So, they agree that if Betty goes to school to study law and becomes a lawyer, he promises not to attempt to kill himself again.[3]

That was the promise and the beginning of everything.

Betty, convinced her brother is innocent, married with two children and now committed to prove her brother's innocence, decides to go back to school to study law, graduate as a lawyer, and get her brother out of jail.

Her time at university was not easy. She suffered divorce, one of her children left her to go live with his dad, as well as the demands required from her college work. During this process, Betty learned about DNA testing that could confirm the blood found at the crime scene wasn't her brother's. Nevertheless, getting old evidence was not an easy task. And, even after proving the DNA was not her brother's, the District Attorney, alleging sufficient additional evidence, refused Kenny's release.

The dream of bringing justice to her brother and winning Kenny's freedom had been destroyed. Even with the scientific evidence of his innocence, they would not release him. This was the moment of death of their hope.

But also that of resurrection.

Betty, obsessed with achieving justice, decided to look for and confront the people that had testified against Kenny. When they were confronted, they confessed with tears in their eyes that Sargent Nancy Taylor, the one who arrested Kenny, had threatened to accuse them of perjury in Kenny's trial if they didn't testify against him.

Having the DNA test in hand and a sworn declaration from the witnesses, Kenny was finally released eighteen years later.

After Betty and Kenny's story was released to the media and it brought Betty fame, she returned to the town and the job she had before she decided to study law. She never again worked as a lawyer, nor earned large paychecks, nor garnered any more fame.

In an article put out by *The New York Times*, Barry Sheck, a lawyer that helped her with the case, said when he found out that Betty had returned to her regular life, "I understand her decision because I got to know her. She never became a lawyer to be a lawyer. She became a lawyer to get her brother out of jail."[4]

Years later, Betty and Kenny's story came to the Hollywood screen in the movie *Conviction* which details the struggles and failures of this real life story.

What I want to make clear is this. If Betty had quit university, or if she had quit when they couldn't access the old evidence showing Kenny's blood, or if she had quit after proving DNA testing found at the scene of the crime scene wasn't his brother's and the District Attorney refused to release him—if she had quit in any of these events—not only would Kenny never have recovered his freedom, but we would have never heard about this amazing story. A story that not only helped Kenny and Betty but helped to generate awareness about the hundreds of cases of people that are imprisoned for crimes they never committed.

When you wonder when you are going to achieve your dream, the answer that should emanate from your heart and soul must be, *when I achieve it*; when you wonder how long you will continue trying, the answer has to be, *when it is accomplished*.

We live in a world where most people don't live their dreams because instead of telling a grand story, they prefer making a grand excuse. Excuses relieve, they show you a way down, back to the ordinary world. The reality is that people who have lived great stories never made excuses. Ever. They have or had an almost obsessive desire to see their dreams come true. They understand that heaven is a good place to rest, not earth, and they devoted all their energy to be able to live out what they wanted.

When you wonder when you are going to achieve your dream, the answer that should emanate from your heart and soul must be, *when I achieve it*; when you wonder how long you will continue trying, the answer has to be, *when it is accomplished.*
#innerherobook.com

The reality is that people who have lived great stories never made excuses.
#innerherobook.com

Without excuse, they kept rowing, they kept looking for publishers that wanted the opportunity to publish a Pulitzer Prize winning piece. They kept struggling against a corrupt system to give freedom to the innocent. They fought and fought and fought until they arrived at the seashore, until they had the prize in their hands, until they saw a brother sleeping in a hotel room, released at last.

I had a hard time thinking how to close such an important chapter as this one. Steven Pressfield's words came to my mind again and again. I decided, then, to close by sharing these words with you:

If you are destined to find the cure for cancer, or write a symphony, or discover cold fusion, but don't do it, you not only harm and destroy yourself, you harm your children, you harm me, and the entire planet.

Never, ever quit building a great story. #innerherobook.com

You shame your guardian angels, you spit on God, who created you and only you with those unique gifts, for the only purpose of making mankind step forward just a millimeter more on their way back to Him.[5]

Never, ever quit building a great story.

CHAPTER 14

VICTORY

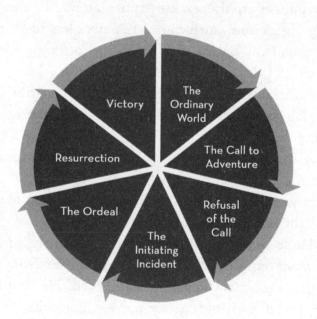

IT WAS MAY 10, 1994. More than four thousand personalities had been invited to this great event and more than a billion people were glued to their televisions with the expectation of witnessing the kind of historic event that would forever change the course of history.

The great Nelson Mandela was taking possession of the presidency of South Africa. In an unexpected twist of history, one of those that can only be explained as happening by divine intervention, in just four years, Mandela went from being a life-prisoner to the first black president to rule the country.

That day in May, hopes for change filled the South African people. For the first time and by popular election, they could start to claim what was always theirs and had been taken away by the authoritarian and evil apartheid.

That day in May was a day of victory.

Hundreds of thousands of people anxiously awaited Mandela to execute the revenge that was certainly merited. Apartheid had been a system to sustain racial segregation, keeping the white minority in power. It created a separation between black and white people whereby whites enjoyed an exclusive position within society, holding the voting rights and much more. For decades, black people had been segregated and outcast with no rights to progress, equality, or democracy.

This regime almost thirty years before that beautiful day in May had sent Nelson Mandela to prison for life, an imprisonment that stole twenty-seven years of his life.

Twenty-seven years in prison. Can you imagine your life if you had to be in jail for twenty-seven years?

Certainly, though many, Mandela would be just the right man to execute the deserved revenge.

But Mandela was not the man that many made him out to be. Mandela was even greater. Years of strife and suffering had turned him into the true man South Africa needed. He understood that vengeance was not what his nation needed, but quite the opposite, a thorough process of national reconciliation.

He made sure that the population of white people were protected and made to feel a part of the nation. He built a coalition in his state body that was totally heterogeneous. During his term, he promoted forgiveness stating that the brave and valiant are not afraid of forgiveness if it serves to promote peace.

Mandela's victory was not in becoming president of South Africa. His victory was what he became in his journey.

Earlier in this book, I've dedicated an entire chapter to treasure. In that chapter, I state that no hero plunges into an adventure without a clear concept of the reward or treasure. No one gets close, not even remotely, to the risk involved in adventure with no vision of the possible reward. In that chapter I discussed your dreams and goals and the power to define them and write them down.

> The real treasure is what you become in your journey. That is the real victory.
> #innerherobook.com

Now, I want to reveal to you the real treasure. It's a treasure that nobody writes about because they don't know about it, or they simply don't care. It's a treasure that is only understood when you look back, not forward. It's a treasure that will not necessarily motivate you to strive day after day. But, one day you will realize that it is the real and most important treasure, the real victory.

The real treasure isn't your goals or dreams. It isn't if you get this or that (although the only way to get it is if you accomplish this or that).

The real treasure is what you become in your journey. That is the real victory.

If Mandela had gained power before being imprisoned, would he have proceeded in the same way he did? I doubt it. Those years in prison were a process of maturity, growth, and understanding of the best way to save South Africa from a civil war. During that time, Mandela could analyze how other African countries had been negatively impacted when white minorities ravaged the nations where they had

> The real treasure is earned in the journey: the real treasure is the journey.
> #innerherobook.com

lost power. He learned that reconciliation was the only way to save his country. Mandela's victory was not the presidency. Mandela's victory was Mandela, the man he had become.

The real treasure is earned in the journey: the real treasure is the journey.

I am not selling you the idea that getting the treasure will be magical or perfect. I am selling you the idea that the journey is what makes life special. Life—and this book, is all about the journey, not the treasure.

Several years ago, I began to realize something interesting. For some reason, which I didn't understand in the beginning, people who had been successful in one area of their lives were able to be successful in other areas much easier than the rest.

I began to study the phenomenon a little bit deeper and discovered a great number of successful athletes that later were successful in business and vice versa. Successful businessmen were able to develop themselves in a sport to an admirable level easily. I noticed how successful artists also made it in other areas of their lives. I realized that high level executives and leaders could fall from grace, only to rise and push their projects and teams once again in a much better way than others. It was like being successful in one area can be easily transferable to another area.

Over time, I learned that success principles, such as discipline, work ethics, persistence, setting goals, visualization, practice, the ability to come back from failures, etc., were exactly the same principles, independent of the area where they wanted to be successful.

> To be successful in one thing is almost a guarantee that you will achieve success in other areas.
> #innerherobook.com

That's why to be successful in one thing is almost a guarantee that you will achieve success in other areas. What you have already learned can be transferred to your next challenge, to your next goal.

This is another example of how the journey is the treasure. When you are victorious, you achieve that sales goal you set, you are able to play that difficult piece of music piece just as you set out to do, you get that promotion you were wanting for so long, or you open that letter that says you've been accepted into a prestigious university. On days like these, you receive much more than that, you hit the culmination of a growth process that is now yours and which nobody can take from you. You have become a different human being. You've grown into a new level. You have something inside of you that you can take wherever you go and fall back on whenever you choose because you have learned the journey, you have learned how to become successful.

Victory is much more than what you have imagined, that's why it's worth striving for.

Remember, in the end, it's not the reward, but it's what you become along the way that you will value with all your heart. So keep moving forward, hero, the world needs you!

> Remember, in the end, it's not the reward, but it's what you become along the way that you will value with all your heart.
> #innerherobook.com

CHAPTER 15

BACK TO THE ORDINARY WORLD

WHEN MY SON BENJAMIN WAS three years old he was a fan of Legos. He got his first Lego set for his third birthday. Two years later, he already had cars, trucks, planes, houses, and even a pizza place in miniature. Allow me to correct myself. At least, he had the pieces that once were cars, trucks, planes, and houses.

At the beginning, when Benjamin got a new box of Legos, I used to sit with him and assemble the pieces in order for him to be able to play. Over time, he developed the ability to assemble them himself, which relegated me to the position of adviser—whom he would conveniently use whenever he didn't have any idea how to finish assembling them.

Then I began to realize that a few days later, all the newly assembled Legos were in pieces in some corner of the house.

I reached the point where I told Benjamin that he wasn't going to receive any more Lego sets until he again assembled the ones he had and kept them that way, without destroying them. Because he was so anxious to get new Lego sets, he started the tough job of reassembling all those he had previously destroyed. Later on, I realized the job was difficult, so I joined in and helped him in the process.

It took us more than six weeks working together to assemble all of the Lego sets. We had to go through the process of collecting all the pieces hidden in every corner of the house, divide them by color, look for and fix the handbooks in order to start the work of rebuilding the collection.

But the day came when all the Lego sets were reassembled: the plane, the cars, the control tower, the gold mine, and the pizza place. Our work had been completed.

Two weeks later, everything was a mess again.

I was furious, and unsure what to do, I asked myself how could my son be so careless to throw away weeks of work? Didn't he learn anything after the slow and arduous work we had done? What was going through his mind the moment he destroyed all his Lego sets? I was completely frustrated.

Some weeks later, I was listening to an interview with Seth Godin, one of the most forward thinkers of our time. While I was listening to him, I received the answer.

It wasn't my son Benjamin's mistake, it was mine. I had transformed a toy designed for adventure, exploration, building, and destroying, into a museum. I had transformed it into something static. I was teaching my son that life has to be lived according to a handbook and when you finish something, you put it on show in order to observe it and show others your work of art.

My son was refusing to be controlled by that way of thinking. Of course, he wanted to assemble the plane, but he also wanted to destroy it and after that, assemble a boat with the remaining pieces. He wanted to assemble a different world every day—today spaceships and planets, tomorrow boats and pirates. He wasn't willing to stay in the ordinary world.

> Don't turn your story into a museum of achievements from the past. Don't fill your life with "those wonderful times."
> #innerherobook.com

In my concept, to destroy something was to waste hours and

days of work. For Benjamin, destruction was an opportunity to start a new adventure. It was the chance to set up a new canvas, white and clean, and ask himself the wonderful question, what do I want to paint today? What do I want to build? Where do I want to travel? What do I want to learn? What am I going to explore?

Being victorious is spectacular. Fulfilling your dream is wonderful. It's good whether you make your business grow to the point where you can fire your boss, or be able to play that musical piece that you thought impossible. It is beautiful when the love of your life tells you, "I accept," when a publisher decides to publish your book. All of that is worth fighting for, and it is a huge satisfaction.

But please don't turn your story into a museum of achievements from the past. Don't fill your life with "those wonderful times." Don't build Lego sets in order to create a museum. Learn to begin again. Sharpen your ear to the new call to adventure.

The hero's journey is a never-ending cycle. The hero's journey is not a summit to reach, but a summit that, when you reach it, shows you new summits in front of you waiting to be conquered.

The return to the ordinary world has an objective, and it is very important that you understand it.

The return to the ordinary world is to celebrate and restore yourself, but not to stay there.

> The hero's journey is a never-ending cycle. The hero's journey is not a summit to reach, but a summit that, when you reach it, shows you new summits that are in front of you waiting to be conquered.
> #innerherobook.com

> The return to the ordinary world is to celebrate and restore yourself, but not to stay there.
> #innerherobook.com

After I climbed Pico Bolivar (the story I recounted of my desire to have my photo taken at the top and then hang next to my uncle's), I came back home with a lot of pictures and stories to tell.

Every time I looked at the pictures, I felt something beautiful reborn inside me. For years, I had the pictures with me wherever I went. Some of them were quite shocking: being in an ice cave, climbing a rock, and, of course, the one at the summit next to the bust of Venezuela's great liberator, Simon Bolivar.

For many years, my love for the mountain was limited to those pictures. Every time I showed them, I felt that I was living the adventure again, but, the reality is, I was living in the past. I was living something that once was, but was no more. There was no new ending, no new call to adventure. There were no new summits to climb or challenges to conquer. I had stayed in the ordinary world.

I am sure that the opposite wouldn't have been fun either. Come back home and start a new adventure right away. There was something special and restorative when I printed my pictures and told family and friends about my adventure. There were laughs, lessons learned, and relationships that grew closer, as usually happens when someone has an adventure to tell.

I also admit that returning home, sleeping in a bed, and taking a hot shower after more than seven days without doing those things was needed—for me and for others. I needed to restore, I needed to remember how good the comforts of the ordinary world feel, and I needed to convince myself that after each adventure, I was going to return there. A good shower, a bed, and hot food are much more enjoyable after an adventure like that one, compared with never daring to go out in search of one.

> The return to the ordinary world is like medicine. In small doses and under doctor orders. #innerherobook.com

But little by little, the good, hot shower is simply a shower and the good food is simply food, and the bed is simply a bed again. Gradually, and probably without noticing, the same days and same routines with the same people and same place begin once again.

And the soul begins to die again.

The return to the ordinary world is like medicine. In small doses and under doctor orders, it will make you feel better, but if you take it in excess, it can kill you.

Remember that your soul cannot live in the ordinary world. The ordinary world doesn't have the kind of oxygen your soul needs. The ordinary world suffocates your soul. Be careful not to get used to it. Be very careful not to lose the love for searching for a new adventure.

> The ordinary world doesn't have the kind of oxygen your soul needs.
> #innerherobook.com

What is your next adventure? It can be taking your dreams to the next level. Maybe you expand your business into new regions with new opportunities, or maybe you learn to play a musical instrument? Or, you finally commit to run your first marathon or give the "yes" to that someone who is asking you to spend the rest of his or her life with you.

Seth Godin, the same man that opened my eyes about the Legos and one of the wisest persons I've ever met, says that he sees life as a series of projects, not unlike a professional career which spans fifty years. Each of those "projects" that Seth mentions—I call them adventures—each of them is a complete cycle of the hero's journey. Even if you decide to spend all your life in the same company or in the same career, you will always be able to learn new things. Force yourself to live new adventures. Start multiple cycles of the hero's journey.

This is the reason why people like you and me will never stop. When you learn to heed the call to adventure, you can never stop. Believe it or not, you and I will

> When you learn to heed the call to adventure, you can never stop.
> #innerherobook.com

never enjoy buying a house with an oceanfront view and live there and lie on the beach for the next twenty years. After a couple of weeks we will be bored and thinking about what we can come up with. We will start wondering what adventure is calling us. We will learn how to fish or plunge the ocean depths to uncover the secrets of the sea. We will take up oil painting, or strike new notes on an old violin. The truth is I don't know what it will be for you or me, but the reality is that we will be looking to start a new cycle of the hero's journey.

And when we have finished that one, we will start another and then another and another…and our lives will be full of moments, experiences, struggles, laughs and stories to tell.

From this day forward, your life will never be the same. Welcome to the life of a hero.

PART FIVE

MY ADVICE
FOR YOUR JOURNEY

CHAPTER 16

GET A MENTOR

RUDY RUETTIGER ACHIEVED WHAT SEEMED IMPOSSIBLE for a boy of his height, physical condition, even his IQ. Ever since he was a boy, he told his family he was going to play football for the University of Notre Dame. Seconds after revealing his dream to his parents and siblings, the house was filled with laughter because of the impossibility of his dream coming true.

Rudy came from a hardworking family that had always worked in an Illinois steel factory. His father had devoted decades of his life working at the factory and his oldest brother had followed in his father's footsteps. The family's expectation was that Rudy would do the same: work a secure job at the steel factory for forty years then enjoy a retirement funded by the Social Security Administration.

And Rudy did it, at least for a while. When he finished college, he started working with his father just as planned. And with him, his best friend, Pete.

One day like all the others, tragedy struck and took Pete's life. His death hit Rudy hard (the initiating incident) and caused him to take the plunge in the adventure of his life: enroll in the prestigious University of Notre Dame and play football.

Quitting his job and moving to South Bend, the town where the campus is located, was just the beginning of the hardest conflict he ever imagined. Sleepless nights and many a night without a place to sleep, multiple rejections in his attempts to be admitted to the university, very little money, and many barriers were only the beginning of the struggles that didn't end even after he was finally admitted to the university.

Once enrolled, his problems continued. Even though he was allowed to practice with the football team, every day he had to face players much taller and more than double his weight. Punches, injuries, and mockery his norm.

However, with time and tenacity, Rudy captured the hearts of his teammates and earned his trainer's respect.

The movie *Rudy*[1] ends at that magical moment in which Rudy is allowed to play for a few seconds in an official Notre Dame football game.

With tears in their eyes, his father, mother, and brother cry when they see him on the field. They cheer from the stands, where they are seated for the first time.

But there is another person in the stands, someone who has sworn to never watch another football game again, but who is there that day to watch Rudy.

Fortune was one of the fundamental pillars to Rudy'success.

I am convinced that Rudy would never have been successful without his help.

Fortune was Rudy's mentor. When Rudy didn't have a job, he helped him. When Rudy didn't have anywhere to sleep, he secretly gave him a key to have access to a room with a bed and bathroom. And one day, when he found Rudy watching the training field from far away because he had decided not to give up, he convinced him not to.

Fortune told Rudy his personal story. He confessed that he himself had given up on making the Notre Dame team many years before, convinced that he would never be allowed to play because of the color of his skin. He explained to him that after quitting, he regretted the decision his entire life and promised Rudy that he would regret it as well if he stuck with his decision to quit.

Rudy would have given up if it weren't for Fortune, if it had not been for his mentor.

Every great story has a mentor. No matter if it's fiction or non-fiction. A mentor is a principle ally that you need on your way. Luke Skywalker in *Star Wars* needs Obi-Wan Kenobi. Frodo and Bilbo in *The Lord of the Rings* and *The Hobbit* needs Gandalf. Every hero, before or in the middle of the conflict, needs a mentor.

> Every hero, before or in the middle of the conflict, needs a mentor.
> #innerherobook.com

You need to have a mentor.

Over the years, I have been blessed to be able to meet extremely successful people, leaders of tens of thousands of people, and I have discovered two aspects as common denominators among all of them. All of them read and each of them have at least one mentor. Having a mentor is an indispensable piece in the puzzle of your life story. It is necessary and part of every great story. A mentor isn't easy to find, but you definitely need one.

There are several reasons why it is necessary to have a mentor. I have listed a few below.

1. A mentor has more knowledge than you. As I have mentioned, back in 2007 I was transferred from Caracas to Cincinnati by Procter & Gamble, the company I was working for at that time. Just being transferred multiplied my salary three-fold. For some weeks, I didn't know what I was going to do with that much money.

I had never lived in the United States, though I had come on vacation several times in the past. There is a difference between living

> Having a mentor is an indispensable piece in the puzzle of your life story.
> #innerherobook.com

in a place compared to when you just go for a vacation. On vacation, everything looks new to you, attractive, and affordable. When you live in a place, it's a different story. Real life and a tourist's life are totally different.

After living a couple of months in the United States, I had a conversation with one of my mentors, Peter Blanco. He recommended I buy a book about personal finance written by the financial genius, Dave Ramsey. He also invested more than one hour explaining to me the difference between the tourist zone and real life here in the US. He was totally clear and honest with me about his mistakes and failures. He told me vividly the consequences his mistakes had brought to his life and gave me honest advice on how to be financially successful in this new country.

The main reason I made certain right decisions with regards to my financial life was precisely because of that conversation with Peter. His advice, experience, and recommendations deeply impacted the life that I live today.

A mentor is a person that has been or is more successful than you in the area where you are looking for guidance. Consequently, their experience and wisdom multiply yours abundantly. Your mentor has made mistakes that you won't make simply by listening and paying attention to their advice.

> A mentor is the key to wisdom, learning from the experience of others.
> #innerherobook.com

Just the way Peter guided me in the financial area, a mentor will guide you to maximize the possibilities of success in the launching of your business, or the writing of your book, or exercising correctly in order to avoid injury. A mentor is the key to wisdom, learning from the experience of others.

2. A mentor has a wider vision than you. When I was nineteen and had already studied two years of university, I was presented with an excellent business opportunity. One year later, I was already making good money and two years after that, a lot of money, leading a group of more than five hundred businessmen, traveling as a speaker to different countries in Latin America and the United States.

When I was twenty-one, I felt my life's dream had come true: money, time, and a touch of fame were much more than I could have ever imagined at that age.

Over time, people started saying that I, a student at Simon Bolivar University, was making more money than the president of the university. Every day, there were more and more comments until I myself started questioning the benefit of even finishing university.

Just to be clear, I don't know if I was making more money than the president of my university, and I don't believe that the reason for studying in a university is to make more money than the highest authority. However, these kind of thoughts feed your ego and can lead you to make wrong decisions.

Every day, I wondered if I really made more money than the president why should I have to finish college? I would be better off dropping my course of studies, focusing on my business, and in about two years, double my income.

Until I got to the point where I really wanted to quit university. Seriously, I had decided to quit studying and dedicate myself to my business.

Thank God I had another mentor, my best mentor on earth. A person that loves me with all of his heart and for whom my best interest will always be his best interest, my father.

If you will allow me to inject a parenthesis here, I would like to say that so many times we think we are the big enchilada, that we have achieved success thanks to ourselves alone and as a result of our own efforts. We forget the key people who are responsible for the success in our lives like our parents, mentors, and various other folks who have opened doors for us, as well as God who granted us the blessing of being alive in the first place.

So now, going back to my story, I was at the point of quitting, had it not been for my father. That evening when he got back from work, we had a conversation while he was getting ready for bed.

This is the way it goes: important conversations happen at unexpected times and places. We would do well to be on the alert for them at all times.

The conversation didn't last long, and there were no tears, but I heard my dad talking to me from the bottom of his heart. Because of him, I decided to finish what I had started, and a couple of years later, we were celebrating my graduation.

I am not saying that studying for a professional career is the way for every single person, but it is important to finish what you start.

For me, it was necessary to finish, to persist, even if my heart wasn't there. Finishing school helped me in every area of my life: my work, my marriage, my relationship with God, and so much more.

But this all happened thanks to a mentor, a person with a bigger vision than mine, a person capable of seeing beyond the money I was making at that moment, a person able to see the big picture, when I was only capable of seeing to the next month.

A mentor has a much wider vision than yours. They understand that sometimes you have to lose in order to win. In an organization, they understand there is a policy, and what appears to be a failure today, will be tomorrow's success. A mentor understands how things are connected, how a little decision in one department affects everything. A mentor understands processes, rewards systems, and the correct incentives to lead an organization and take it forward.

Do you want to become a visionary person? Get a mentor. Become a follower. Every hero needs a mentor.

3. A mentor holds you accountable. Like I said before, a mentor is more successful than you in the area in which you are needing his or her advice. Consequently, mentors don't like to waste their time. They invest their time and energy in people they realize have potential and are willing to do what they need to do in order to be successful.

A mentor doesn't accept excuses. He was there before you, and overcoming excuses was the reason for his success. A mentor won't accept your excuses.

The mentor-hero relationship is not always a bed of roses. I remember on many occasions trying to cancel meetings with my mentor to avoid being confronted. Nevertheless, that fear of being confronted helped me take the next step and move forward. The fear of doing what I had to do was less than the fear I felt standing before my mentor empty-handed.

Finding a mentor is difficult. Losing a mentor is easy. Having one commits you to do what you have to do in order to achieve success. A mentor will ask you to apologize to your wife even if you are not guilty, write a page of your book even if you don't feel like it, go out and present your business plan or sell your product one more time, even if you feel like there is no hope.

4. A mentor has more connections than you. The world moves by personal connections. Many times we think we can create processes to avoid dealing with the lack of objectivity of human beings, but the reality is that human relationships move the world.

I am pretty sure that it is a thousand times more likely that you'll buy a product or service if it comes recommended by your best friend than from hearing about it in a magnificent piece of advertisement on TV or the Internet. Word of mouth was, is, and, will always be the most powerful advertisement because it is based on human relationships.

The connections you have will open doors that you would have never imagined. And your mentor has many more connections than you.

This book that you are reading now is the product of a connection. My mentor, Andres Panasiuk, introduced me to Larry Downs, a senior vice-president and publisher at HarperCollins Christian Publishing. However, I'm not saying the simple fact of having that connection made the publication of this book possible. There were also years of effort put into building my platform, months of struggling to make a strong and interesting publishing proposal, and lots of hours with no sleep writing these lines.

But everything became a reality thanks to Andres introducing me to Larry, and Larry counted on me for the production of this book. Andres opened a door to me that few have access to. Hundreds of thousands of manuscripts are rejected in the United States every year. The vast majority are not even read because no publishing company is able to read them all. However, mine got into the hands of a vice-president thanks to my mentor.

> A mentor has connections. #innerherobook.com

A mentor has connections. Sometimes, he has many of them. And if you show your mentor your commitment to success, he can open doors for you as needed.

5. A mentor can become one of your best friends. It's difficult for me not to feel a life commitment with Peter Blanco, Andres Panasiuk, my father, my mother, and many others for their wise counsel, for being there when I needed them the most, for opening doors and introducing me to key people along my journey. Having a mentor activates the circle of love: giving without expecting. Having a mentor is the closest experience that I have had of what God is to us, giving without expecting anything in return.

> A good mentor fights and hopes for your success. Relationships that are made during the journey often become the deepest ones in your life. #innerherobook.com

Many times, I have wondered why many of them do what they do, why they decided to help me when they don't get any benefit in return.

The answer is that they are demonstrating by giving of themselves with their lives what real love is.

This deep desire to reciprocate all the benefit received, builds the most beautiful relationships. Your mentors many times end up being your greatest friends.

A good mentor fights and hopes for your success. Relationships that are made during the journey often become the deepest ones in your life, which I am pretty sure you will value more than success itself.

You'll remember that I told you this when that moment comes.

God as a Mentor

I can't finish this chapter without referring to the mentor of mentors, to the sole owner of past, present, and future, the One that has endless wisdom and is capable of opening or closing any door. Our Creator.

God is gigantic, infinite, and impossible to comprehend totally. That's why I am not going to box Him into only one role, but I can certainly say that one of God's roles is to be your mentor. God loves you deeply in the same way that a father or a mother love their children. In the same way that I am sure that my father wanted me to have the conversation with him instead of someone else about quitting university or not, God wants you to talk to him every day to guide you, instruct you, confront you, and encourage you in your journey.

There is no greater fulfillment than when you connect with your Creator through prayer, meditation, and reading his Word. A mentor will give you strength from the outside in and from from the inside out.

I want you to live a great story, but I also want you to get to know your Creator in a profound way. Even more, I can't conceive of how you can live a great story without having God on your side.

> A mentor will give you strength from the outside in and from from the inside out.
> #innerherobook.com

One of the most important points of this book is living a great story, a story that is worth living and telling. I want you to know that there is also another great story you are inside of, one even greater that is happening right now. It is the story of the redemption and reconciliation between God and his world. Between God and you.

Looking to God and his Son as your mentors will show you something extraordinary—how your sweeping story connects to a much larger and greater one, God's story.

Separation from God and forfeiting his Word and commandments, will cause you to live an empty and inconsequential story. Conversely, understanding and knowing our Creator will give you the opportunity to live a profoundly rewarding story and be part of the much larger plan of redemption and reconciliation with the world.

> God is the mentor of mentors. There is no greater wisdom than his.
> #innerherobook.com

Don't stop looking for Him until you connect and become reconciled today. Remember this great truth: God is the mentor of mentors. There is no greater wisdom than his.

CHAPTER 17

CREATE A COMMUNITY

SAN FRANCISCO BECAME ONE OF my favorite cities when I had the opportunity to visit for the first time back in 2014. It wasn't only for the beauty of its landscape, the Golden Gate Bridge, or Alcatraz, but for the perfect union of a culture on the cutting edge of technology with a passion for nature and all things organic and authentic.

I went to San Francisco for work reasons. My job was to get together with a particular group of people for whom we were designing a product. We wanted to understand their needs, wishes, and frustrations to make sure our design gave them what they were really after.

The meetings were long, each one of them running about three hours each. When we left one meeting, the driver was ready to take us to the next.

My driver's name was Mikkael. He was from Ukraine, but he had lived in San Francisco for more than thirty years. Mikkael ended up being a very special person for me on that work trip. Despite of being in San Francisco for work, he made me feel like I was on vacation. Between meetings, he told me everything he knew about

San Francisco, and he stopped at every important point along the way that he could. Thanks to Mikkael, I learned a lot about that beautiful city.

One afternoon, leaving my last meeting for the day, Mikkael decided to drive me to Muir Woods National Monument about thirty minutes from the city. Mikkael told me that I couldn't leave San Francisco without seeing the tallest trees in the world, the giant redwoods.

The experience of standing in front of one of those trees is difficult to explain. Comparing my life span to that of a red Sequoyah is the closest I have come to understanding my temporal condition in this world.

The redwood trees are the tallest trees in the world. They can reach a height of more than three hundred feet. This is comparable to a building of more than thirty floors. Their diameter can be more than twenty-five feet. These trees can live more than two thousand years.

The interesting thing about these trees is that their roots are not as big or as deep as one would think. They grow no more than two inches in diameter and don't even grow very deep. According to physics, it is impossible that a tree like that could sustain itself.

The key is that the redwood interweaves its roots with other trees around it. Hundreds and thousands of roots are intertwined creating a huge network that allows it to stand, thanks to the combined strength of the others.

A redwood tree cannot stand by itself. It only stands in community.

The greatest living creature on the planet can't sustain itself by its own means, it needs a network of other trees around it that supports one another. These trees have survived intense fires (in fact, some of them still bear the marks), typhoons, storms, floods, and everything they have endured because they have each other.

Although the erroneous perception exists that the hero is a lone, solitary individual, the reality is that no one in this world needs more community support than someone who is on the adventure of his life.

You and I need a community, a group of heroes of both men and women who are struggling each day through their journey. We don't necessarily need people who are walking our same journey with the same dreams, same goals, same business or industry, but simply people who are walking out journey.

It was a Monday at 3:00 in the morning when my alarm clock rang. This time, I didn't have to go to the airport. It was the signal to get together with my community. Every other week at 3:00 a.m., I turn on my computer and Skype with my group. Some of them live in Spain and some in other countries, which is the reason for the strange hour. But it doesn't matter. What I am looking for is the power of community. Every two weeks when we get together,

> Although the erroneous perception exists that the hero is a lone, solitary individual, the reality is that no one in this world needs more community support than someone who is on the adventure of his life.
> #innerherobook.com

we chat about our projects, our goals, and we make a commitment to the group to what we are going to do the following two weeks, and then we dedicate some time for feedback.

As you can see, you don't need to be in the same city or the same country. If you can meet in person, that is marvelous. If not, that's great too. The important thing is that you create a community of heroes, a group of people that have made the decision to leave the ordinary world and have accepted their call to adventure.

I can also tell you about another community that is even more special. While I was writing this book, I received devastating news. One of those that hits you so hard you don't even know what happened. I instantly understood that I was going to go through a long and deep conflict. I immediately called a group of five people, a community of people to guide me, give me encouragement, and pray fervently for me in my new struggle. The most beautiful thing about all of this is that I received deep love, compassion, and commitment from that group to be there for me, praying with me each and every day. That is a community of heroes.

> A band of heroes will help you not to fall into the temptation of going back to the ordinary world or give up in your struggle.
> #innerherobook.com

You need to start creating that community of heroes in your life. Both you and I need to invest time and energy to make it a reality.

This community of heroes will start creating a network of roots that can't be seen, that are underground. That network of roots will make us support one another in the hardest times. Remember that life will always invite you back to the ordinary world. Along your journey, there will always be a downhill shortcut where rest, pleasure, and comfort are promised. A band of heroes will help you not to fall into the temptation of going back to the ordinary world or give up in your struggle. There will be times when the roots are so strong that even if you want to go back, you won't be able to. Your community of heroes will maintain you on your own hero's journey.

> Your community of heroes will maintain you on your own hero's journey.
> #innerherobook.com

CHAPTER 18

LEARN TO DEFINE WHAT IS ESSENTIAL

SOME YEARS AGO, I RECEIVED an e-mail that showed the market strategy for winning one of P&G's well-known brands. When I opened the document, I quickly noticed that it consisted of more than 120 pages, which immediately convinced me that I was not about to read it.

However, I decided to give the first few pages a quick glance before going over the last two which were under the title, "Conclusions and Recommendations."

The first point that I read really caught my attention. This point indicated the main strategy in making a profit: "We need to make a profit for all of our products (for brand X)."

This fact did more harm than good to the organization. How can we make a profit in everything? What is the priority? If resources dwindle, as they always do, where do we put our focus?

Throughout my life, I have seen a lot of managers, businessmen and people in general with this kind of thinking. They believe they can make a profit in everything.

The reality is that you need to choose your battles. You must decide what you need in order to win and what you are willing to lose. What you need to say "no" to so you can say "yes" to others.

A case worthy of admiration is Southwest Airlines. They have an extremely clear business model and know what they will say yes to and what they will say no to. They know that they won't be successful in everything, but they are clear in which things they will win at, and their success continues to grow.

> You must decide what you need in order to win and what you are willing to lose. What you need to say "no" to so you can say "yes" to others.
> #innerherobook.com

Contrary to the most common model for commercial airlines, which offers almost world-wide destinations, and multiple aircrafts, and a variety of food, TV, etc., Southwest Airlines only offers a limited number of destinations, one kind of aircraft, with all extras eliminated. Because of this decision, they are able to lower their overall operating costs in a significant way and offer very competitive prices. The result is an airline that generates profits and growth year after year in a world where other airlines are bleeding financially. The skilled leadership at Southwest Airlines, building a company based on just the essentials, has brought them tremendous success.

As I mentioned before, Starbucks was forced to return to their essentials in order to survive and keep growing.

We need to learn how to trim. We need to go back to the essentials.

> Essentialism is not about doing more things, it is about doing the right things.
> #innerherobook.com

In his excellent book *Essentialism: The Disciplined Pursuit of Less,* Greg McKeown defines essentialism as the discipline of doing things right. Regarding this he says:

The way of the essentialist...consists in pausing constantly to ask yourself, "Am I investing in the right activities?"

Essentialism is not about doing more things it is about doing the right things. Neither does it mean doing less just for the sake of doing less. It is about investing time and energy in the most intelligent possible way to provide our greatest contribution just doing what is essential... The way of the essentialist rejects the idea that we can take care of everything, but rather, asks us to struggle with «lose to win» deals and make difficult decisions.[1]

One of the greatest risks that exists after you learn and apply the hero's journey to your life is that you can begin multiple journeys simultaneously erroneously believing that they will all eventually lead to victory.

One of the most important lessons for all heroes, and one we have already discussed in our chapter on treasure, is the need to clarify what you want and to focus on the essential activities that will lead you to your destination. If you are not focused, you can fall into what is known as the paradox of success.

> One of the most important lessons for all heroes is the need to clarify what you want and to focus on the essential activities that will lead you to your destination.
> #innerherobook.com

The Paradox of Success

The paradox of success is a process that shows how being successful can lead you to failure if you don't focus on the essential, which is what brought you success in the first place. This is the process:

Phase 1: We have clarity of purpose. We put great effort into critical activities in order to be successful in reaching our goal. Focus and persistence allow us to begin having success.

Phase 2: Our success is beginning to be noticed by others. We start to grow and become experts. People seek us out for consultation and advice.

Phase 3: Many opportunities open up to us thanks to our success. We need to focus more on managerial-type activities than before. Other activities relating to being an expert start to demand our time and energy.

Phase 4: We get distracted from the activities that brought us success in the first place. Our momentum begins to decay and we start losing the success that we once had. Our success becomes the reason for our failure.

I remember when I started a direct-sales business that brought me a lot of success. My daily enthusiasm energized me to present the business plan and product line with discipline and persistence.

Over time, my company grew to hundreds of distributors. With financial success also came commitments to the organization. Then came recognition and opportunities as a speaker for other organizations. These opportunities caused me to lose focus on the initial activities that had brought me success because I was taking advantage of the other opportunities that earned money and brought recognition.

In time, the growth momentum of my company slowed down and before long began to stagnate. In the end, the success that I once had, led me to failure because of my inability to choose what was essential on my journey.

Learning to define what is essential and keep yourself committed to the discipline of executing those activities and not falling into the temptation of new opportunities will be one of the pillars of sustained success on your journey. One of the greatest examples of focusing on the essentials I learned when I read about Jim Sinegal. Jim is one of the founders of Costco, a wholesale chain-store that has gross sales of more than one hundred billion dollars a year.

Besides being the founder, Jim was also the CEO of the company until 2011 and is one of the most admired CEOs in the entire world. He was named by *Business Week* as one of the best managers of 2003. He was also named by *Time* magazine one of the most influential men in the world. And, for more than twelve years he has been named one of the most respected CEOs by *Barron's*.[2]

During his time as CEO, and in spite of having the regular activities of a CEO at that level, he always understood that visiting the stores, including walking around the sales floor, was essential in order to be in touch with the business and to make sure his vision was being made into a reality.

Now when I say that visiting the stores was considered essential, it makes sense for a business that has two, three, or four stores. It also makes sense if all the stores are in the same city or the same region. However, Jim used to personally travel to more than two hundred stores every year between the United States, Canada, Mexico, Europe, Japan, and Australia. Visiting two hundred stores per year means you spend most of your time on a plane and walking around store aisles, talking to employees, and checking merchandise.

For Jim Senegal, investing most of his time doing that was much more important than long meetings in corporate offices. It was an essential that he demonstrated all his life as leader of that enormous organization.

Mountain lovers understand this concept well. I remember my first trip to the mountains when I had to pack my first backpack with several days' worth of necessary hiking supplies. The first time you prepare a backpack, you think that it's something simple. If you're going to be on the mountain for five days, you need five changes of clothes, food, equipment, and all your grooming items, an extra change of clothes for an emergency, a couple of sweaters, a pair of pajamas, etc.

Everything is fine until you put the backpack on and feel the weight that compresses the bones in your spine. You realize right then that you won't be able to walk for more than an hour with that much weight on your back.

Those are the moments in which some friend or a more experienced mountain guy looks at you and laughs. He takes everything out of your backpack and starts teaching you what is really essential. You only need a few of your grooming items and one t-shirt that you will use for the five days. Forget about underwear. He removes clothing labels. He even breaks the toothbrush handle so that you don't have to carry it. He minimizes all the possible weight. He puts in your backpack only the essentials. He uses a minimalist process.

Most of the time, we live our lives with a bunch of unnecessary items—telephones, vehicles, houses, equipment, meetings, commitments, activities. We live our lives as if we were carrying a backpack with one hundred pounds on our back compressing our bones with every step. We feel suffocated to the point that we can't enjoy the vistas of the road because of the pain caused by the load we're bearing.

How would our lives be if we only carried the essentials? How would we walk our hero's journey if we were lighter? Can you imagine a life with few commitments, without the unnecessary things or activities that add little value to us? What would your life be like if you learned how to say no?

Never forget that society, family, and friends will constantly try to determine what success is for you. The greatest mistake you can make is to live your life trying to comply with other's expectations just to get to the end of your days and realize that the ladder you were going up was leaning against the wrong wall.

> The greatest mistake you can make is to live your life trying to comply with others' expectations
> #innerherobook.com

One of our greatest problems is we're not designed to eliminate but increase. We go grocery shopping to fill the refrigerator and the pantry without eliminating first what we don't need. We buy new garments without eliminating old ones. We add new responsibilities to our lives without prioritizing and eliminating what is not producing good results any more.

My goal in this chapter is to convince you that the process of eliminating will change your life. It will make you a hundred times more productive and will help you achieve what you really want in life.

This concept is part of The Pareto Principle discovered by Wilfredo Pareto.

Wilfredo Federico Pareto was an Italian engineer, economist, and sociologist who discovered the 80/20 principle. He discovered 80% of Italian land belonged to 20% of the population.

The 80/20 principle has been applied to many areas of society, businesses, time and resource management, among others.

Here are some examples:

Time: 20% of our time produces 80% of the results.
Products: 20% of your products is responsible for 80% of the sales.
Reading: 20% of a book has 80% of its content. (I hope that isn't true for this book, but that you feel every page holds value).
Work: 20% of your work/projects contribute to 80% of the result.
Customers: 20% of your customers represent 80% of your sales.

Analyzing the concept from a general point of view, indicates the following. Eighty percent of results come from twenty percent of the effort. In other words, the other eighty percent of the effort that you put into it only brings twenty percent of the results.

After the twenty percent of activity that brings you eighty percent of the results, what remains is called the point of diminishing returns in which the more effort you put in, the lower the results you get.

The key is to detect the important activities that constitute the twenty percent, and after that eliminate the rest.

One thing you don't want to lose sight of is that the final goal is not just eliminating but replacing the time, effort, and resources with more productive activities. Activities that get you where you want to go.

This process of elimination will free up space, time, and resources in your life that will allow you to reinvest them in reflection, imagination, innovation, and activities that will accelerate you to your dreams or even make time—in quality and quantity—for the people that you love the most.

Remember this. Learn to travel light. Don't allow you or anyone else to put heavy things in your backpack. Focus on the twenty percent that will give you the eighty percent of the results. Don't carry around weight when you walk. You don't need as many things as you think, and people won't mind that you tell them no. Enjoy the journey.

> Remember this. Learn to travel light.
> #innerherobook.com

CHAPTER 19

LEARN TO PICK FLOWERS ALONG THE WAY

ON A COLD MORNING in January, a man entered a subway station in Washington, D.C. and started playing an old violin. It was almost eight in the morning, rush hour for the train, and hundreds of people were hurrying to get to their jobs.

The man played six pieces lasting about forty-five minutes. During that time, more than a thousand people passed by him, of which only seven stopped for a few seconds to listen and then go on their way. Close to twenty people gave him a tip, which means this man earned a little more than thirty-two dollars for his performance.

Except for a woman who listened to him for about two minutes, the rest listened no more than thirty seconds, then kept walking. When he was done, the man put away his violin and left the subway station. Nobody noticed, nobody applauded, and there was no recognition.

What no one knew is that this violinist was Joshua Bell, one of the greatest violinists in the entire world. A man who three days before had filled a theater, where each ticket was worth more than one hundred dollars. Not only that, but he was playing a violin made in 1713 by Antonio Stradivarius worth more than three and a half million dollars.

Among the six pieces that Joshua Bell played was "Chaconne" by Bach, which is considered one of the most difficult pieces in the world. For forty-five minutes, more than one thousand people walked past of one of the best violinists in the world, playing one of the most difficult pieces in the world, with one of the most expensive violins ever made. And, only seven people had stopped to listen.[1]

This is a true story. It was an experiment organized by the *Washington Post* to try and understand perception, tastes, and priorities in human beings. That's why he went undercover to one of the most crowded places in the city. Would people be able to stop and appreciate beauty?

While they were planning the experiment, Leonard Slatkin, Musical Director of the National Orchestra, commented that he was sure a multitude of people would stop to listen and that Bell would collect at least one hundred and fifty dollars minimum. But the reality is that there was no multitude and neither was there much money.

One of the conclusions of the experiment was the following. If we don't have a moment to stop, recognize, and listen to one of the most acclaimed musicians in the world playing one of the most complex music pieces of history, what other things are we missing?

Both you and I are living in a world that moves quickly. We live most of the time absorbed by daily activities and commitments that we have to meet. We are in a rat-race where we run and run on the wheel without realizing that there is a world offering up gifts of beauty right in front of our eyes each and every day.

What are you missing?

I believe both God and life give us Joshua Bell musical pieces played on million dollar violins every day, and we simply pass them by because we have something urgent to do.

The hero's journey never ends. It is a cycle that will cause you to wake up your inner hero, accomplish your dreams, and live a life worth living. But we can't forget that the beauty of life is in its moments. We can't focus so much on the future that we neglect the present. We can't miss Joshua Bell playing beautiful music when we cross paths with him.

Several years ago, I wanted to show my son a stream that I had discovered in the park close to our house. I told him about the little river, and I promised that I would take him that afternoon.

When we got to the park, I put my son on my shoulders, and we started our adventure through the woods toward the river.

I had walked less than ten steps when my son who was just learning to talk told me, "Daddy, I want flower, I want flower," referring to a wildflower beside the road. I crouched down, picked it, and gave it to him.

We kept walking and two steps later he saw another flower and told me, "Daddy, look at flower. I want flower." I crouched down, helped him pick it, and then he said, "Daddy, look, another one and another one!"

At that moment, I was thinking that I couldn't stop every two steps to pick flowers, so I told him, "Son, we won't make it to the river on time. Please remember that we are going to the river." It didn't surprise me when he paid no attention to what I said but kept asking for all the flowers that he found along the way.

After more than thirty minutes and so many stops to pick flowers that I lost count, we finally got to the river.

But, the river was dry.

A severe drought the weeks prior had dried the river up. The stream had been reduced to an imperceptible trickle of water and piles of rocks.

Frustrated, I turned back and started walking toward the park. And as one would expect, my son started to find all the flowers that he had missed on the way to the river and, of course, I had to stop, bend down, and pick the flowers, and give them to him while still carrying him on my back.

When we came out of the woods, I was completely frustrated, but when I looked at my son I noticed that he wasn't. In fact, he looked immensely happy.

His little hands were full of flowers.

For him, it had been the best event of the day, picking flowers with his dad.

This is exactly what happens in life. We set a goal for ourselves or set ourselves an objective. We want to be successful in our business. We want the promotion at work. We want that car or this house or some other thing.

And many times, when we get there, it turns out that the river is dry, and we get frustrated.

And we believe the solution is in the next river.

For my son, life is different. For my son, the pleasure is in discovering how beautiful life is, the new things for him, what he hasn't yet seen. What sometimes both you and I have stopped paying attention to, or we have even forgotten, is that it is there for us.

For my son life is about the flowers, the birds, the moon, the stars, and the sun.

I want to make sure you know something. You will reach your goal. You will fulfill your dream. If you are determined, persistent, and consistent you will make it. The objective of sharing the hero's journey with you is so that you are able to understand the process, where you are now, and where you want to go.

You will be victorious. It may be you get there sooner or later than expected. But, it's important that you are convinced you will make it.

Learn how to develop the essential ability to look ahead while stopping to pick and smell the flowers.

#innerherobook.com

But the truth is that sometimes, without knowing it, we set goals we believe will bring us happiness and yet many times they are dry rivers. That's why, and just in case you get there and realize the river is dry, don't forget to notice, pick and smell the flowers along your way.

And when you get to the end of your life, no matter how much you have achieved, or what you've become, at the end of it all, your hands will be full of flowers.

Don't forget to live in the present. Live life now and enjoy Joshua Bell's melody and the beautiful wildflowers that God gives you along the way. Learn how to develop the essential ability to look ahead while stopping to pick and smell the flowers.

As Facundo Cabral said, "We are born to live, that's why the most important resource that we have is time. Our passage through this planet is so short that it's a bad idea not to enjoy every step and every moment, with the blessing of a mind that has no limits and a heart that is able to love much more than what we think."[2]

CHAPTER 20

CREATE HABITS AND WATCH THEM WORK FOR YOU

WHAT WE BECOME AT THE end of our journey depends greatly on the little actions we make day to day. Great successes and disasters are neither built nor destroyed by massive effort in a short period of time but by little efforts and everyday actions that eventually build great and inconceivable things.

Some time ago, I found this poem on the Internet. I went through an exhaustive search to locate the author, but I couldn't find anything, so I share it with you from an unknown pen:

> What we become at the end of our journey depends greatly on the little actions we make day to day.
> #innerherobook.com

I am your constant companion.
I am your greatest helper or heaviest burden.
I will push you onward or drag you down to failure.

I am completely at your command.
Half the things you do, you might as well turn over to me,
And I will do them—quickly and correctly.
I am easily managed; you must be firm with me.

Show me exactly how you want something done,
And after a few lessons, I will do it automatically.
I am the servant of great people,
And alas, of all failures as well.
Those who are great, I have made great.
Those who are failures, I have made failures.

You may run me for profit or run me for ruin;
It makes no difference to me.

Take me, train me, be firm with me
And I will place the world at your feet.
Be easy with me and I will destroy you.

Who am I? I am Habit![1]

One of my best friends is Alberto Jimenez. He is passionate about God and also aviation. Ever since he was little his dream was to fly, until finally, he became a pilot. Alberto is one of those guys that when he is not working flying an aircraft, he is playing with a flight simulator at home. That is to say, when he is not working he is playing at work.

One day, when we met each other on a trip I made to Florida. He invited me for a ride in the plane that he flies. For maintenance reasons, he had to fly the plane for a specified time, so he invited me and my family to take a ride through the heavens over Miami.

I felt like a millionaire that day going to a private airport and getting on a private jet where every seat was first class. Every detail of the plane spoke of luxury. Travelling like that would make anyone want to travel.

Another interesting thing was that I had the chance to be close to the cabin and I was able to watch the take-off and landing just the way a pilot does. I also had the chance to see the thousand things that Alberto did and ask him about every detail to the satisfaction of my curiosity.

One of the interesting things that he explained to me was that after putting the flight plan in the plane system, which includes entering the code of the departing airport, the arrival airport, flight altitude, taking off and reaching the desired altitude, he set the aircraft to autopilot.

> Drop by drop, water breaks the stone.
> #innerherobook.com

Autopilot takes the aircraft to its desired destination, maintaining a pre-determined altitude. Just before landing, the pilot takes control of the airplane again.

Something that really caught my attention is that the autopilot is a great help if, and only if, you define clearly the flight plan. That is, where you want to go, how you want to get there, and when you want to get there. If you don't have a clear flight plan, the autopilot is useless and even dangerous.

The reality of life is that whether we want it or not, all of us have an autopilot of sort activated. The problem is that if we don't have a clear flight plan we end up in a totally different place from the one we wanted.

This autopilot is our habits.

We all are controlled by our habits. If habits didn't exist, we would have to think before taking any action all the time. Habits help us to unload our conscious minds about the automatic decisions that need to be made.

> After you transform an activity into a habit you don't need to think about it anymore; you don't need to struggle.
> #innerherobook.com

Drop by drop, water breaks the stone. Your habits will make you a healthy or unhealthy person; a prosperous or poor person; a person with lots of friends or a lonely person. Day after day habits define your destiny.

If we are able to control our habits, they will take us where we want to go. Creating a new positive habit is not an easy job but it is the best investment that you can make in your lifetime. After you transform an activity into a habit you don't need to think about it anymore; you don't need to struggle. It will happen automatically for you.

There is a lot of research attempting to discover the time needed to develop a habit. I have heard from twenty-one days to six weeks. In my personal experience, twenty-one days has not been enough, but thirty-one days has been perfect. I will explain to you the process of developing a habit.

Days one to three: During those first days, carrying out the activity that we want to develop as a habit is extremely easy. That activity is managed by our enthusiasm. We wake up early to read, meditate, or exercise. Enthusiasm gives us energy and motivation to do what we need to do.

Days four to seven: Days of extreme effort. During these days, we need to use every ounce of our willpower. If we start exercising, our muscles hurt. Getting up early to read or write is not as easy as before. At this point is when most people quit.

Days eight to fourteen: Days of medium effort. Although it is still difficult, it is a little bit easier than before. We start noticing that some days we feel excited and some days, we don't.

Days fifteen to twenty-one: Days of low effort. The habit is starting to take shape. Inertia working against us is losing power. We start feeling like we are in control.

Day twenty-one: Moment of zero inertia. This is the moment that we were waiting for. Inertial force that didn't let us get up early, eat healthy, or exercise has been beaten. The great mistake that we can make at this point is to give up. The habit hasn't been created yet; we have just beaten inertia. The habit will be fully created in the days ahead.

Days twenty-two to thirty-one: Creation of positive inertia and momentum. Establishing the habit. These are the golden days. These are the days in which you are writing your destiny. You need to put special effort to continue building the habit at this moment. If you are careless, inertia can turn around and attack you again.

Day thirty-one: The habit has been created.

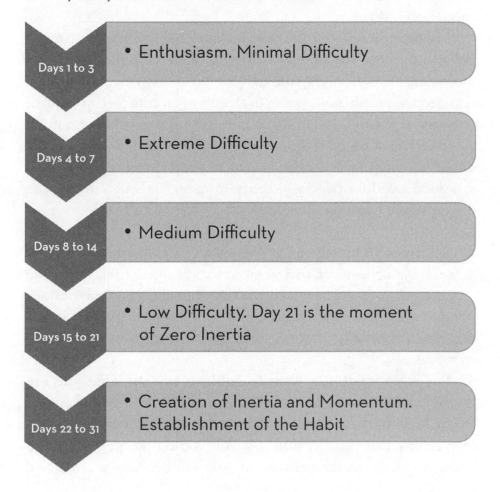

Days 1 to 3
- Enthusiasm. Minimal Difficulty

Days 4 to 7
- Extreme Difficulty

Days 8 to 14
- Medium Difficulty

Days 15 to 21
- Low Difficulty. Day 21 is the moment of Zero Inertia

Days 22 to 31
- Creation of Inertia and Momentum. Establishment of the Habit

Now that you know the process of creating habits, it is important that you develop healthy habits, habits that will take you to your destiny. Here are six tips that have been key for developing positive habits in my life and also to get rid of habits that were taking me away from my destiny.

1. Connect the change you want to make, to your treasure. It is important to understand that there is an infinite number of positive habits, such as exercising, meditating, and praying, even drinking green tea in the morning. It is common for people start working on good habits just for the simple fact that they're good habits, without connecting them to the treasure that they're looking for on the journey of their lives. In the long run, this can bring frustration and failure.

For example, if your life plan includes being a healthy person, you can fall into the mistake of trying to develop the habits of a professional athlete, taking the activities to an extreme. If your plan is to become an athlete, develop the habits of an athlete. If your plan, however, is just to be a healthy person, get used to habits that make you healthier at the level that you want to get. Not everybody needs to run ten kilometers per day. For some people, the habit of hiking at a good speed for twenty or thirty minutes is enough to take the person where he or she wants to get.

2. Start today. One of the biggest traps for our mind is procrastination. When we are convinced that we need to add a new habit to our life or leave behind a negative one, the first thought that comes to our mind is to start next week, next month, or by January 1st. This is self-deception. Start today. Make adjustments along the way.

3. Focus on what you want to achieve, not on what you are trying to eliminate. Most of the time, we focus on what we are trying to eliminate, instead of looking at what we want to achieve. Don't think that the diet plan that you chose is keeping you from eating, think about the person that you will become as a result of establishing the habit of eating healthy.

Remember, don't focus on the sacrifice. Focus on the achievement. Your journey will be much easier.

4. Focus on just a few changes at a time. One of the most common mistakes is people decide to change their entire life overnight.

They decide they can't stand living that way and quit smoking, start eating healthy, register at a gym, get a good book to start reading again, throw out the TV, and donate ten percent of their income to a noble cause.

The brutal reality is that, with few exceptions, these people don't achieve results and return to old habits in no time.

The key is not to forget bad habits develop little by little over time and have been in place for many months or even years. In the same way, we need to start developing the good ones, little by little, one at a time.

Regardless of the fact that you want to change everything in your life, start with one or two habits until you have control of them. After that, add another one and make the change little by little. Remember that it is not a race, it's your life journey.

5. Be precise about what habit you want to develop. Making up your mind to develop ambiguous habits is not very helpful. For example, developing the habit of generosity is ambiguous. Developing the habit of donating to your church, charity, or a needy person is more a precise habit.

Becoming healthier? Ambiguous. Walking for thirty minutes for five days a week? Much better. Developing a deeper spiritual life? Ambiguous. Praying together as a family before going to bed every night in thanksgiving for that day that was granted to us? Much better.

Make sure to specify what the action is that you need to make in the habit.

6. Create a support ecosystem. With the goal of eating healthier, my wife and I decided to eliminate processed carbohydrates from our diet six days a week. Saturday is our reward day, and we can eat whatever we want.

How do we develop a support ecosystem? We don't buy carbohydrates when we go grocery shopping. I bring my lunch to work from home, saving money and getting rid of the temptation of slipping from the diet plan. We support each other in the hard moments, etc.

What I want to make clear is that you need to develop an atmosphere that makes the creation of the habit easier and keeps you away from the temptation to go back. Here are some very interesting examples that I have seen:

- Get rid of credit cards and dump them in order to become debt-free.
- Go to bed in your exercise clothing to be ready when you get up the next day.
- Place the alarm clock far from your bed in order to make you get up when you need to.
- Turn off the cell phone when you get home in order to avoid distractions with trivial things like social networks or e-mails.
- Park the car several blocks away from your workplace to make yourself walk.

Remember what I told you before. Water, drop by drop, breaks the rock. Your habits will make you a healthy or unhealthy person, prosperous or poor, surrounded by friends or lonely. Habits define your destiny day after day.

Create habits and then you can go to bed.

> **Create habits and then you can go to bed.**
> **#innerherobook.com**

CHAPTER 21

DEVELOP A LOVE FOR READING

I DISCOVERED READING WHEN I was nineteen. Before that, I was a functional illiterate. I used to read only when it was necessary and only subjects that I needed to learn in order to graduate from university. At that age, a new world was opened before my very eyes.

The first book I read was *The 7 Habits of Highly Effective People* by Dr. Stephen Covey. This book changed my life, not only because of the information it gave me, but from the discovery that all that wisdom was at my service for the rest of my life between the covers of a good book.

After that book, I read another one, and then another one, and so on. I started to realize something interesting: I could become one of the best in the world in any area that I so desired, if I committed to reading. Why? Because most people don't read. I discovered that reading gave me a magnificent competitive advantage in any field I desired to venture into.

Just by reading a couple of books on the same subject, I had more knowledge about that specific subject than ninety percent of others. I was amazed that people didn't want to read, and I couldn't understand why they were so willing to ignore so much potential for wisdom and growth.

I once heard someone say where you will be in ten years will depend on the people you're associating with and the books that you're reading. Reading, or not reading, is one of the elements that will define your journey.

From the time I was nineteen, now fifteen years later, I have read hundreds of books. That's why I want to give you some advice that I believe will help in the process of reading.

1. Read books, not only blogs, newspapers, and magazines. Reading blogs, newspapers, and magazines is important, but should never take the place of a book. Blogs, newspapers, and magazines are short publications, which are perfect for certain types of information, but a good book takes you to deeper levels of understanding never found in the short content that you get from your favorite blog.

Here are some of the benefits that books provide over shorter publications:

- They develop your ability to analyze and understand problems. Most of us are inundated with news that informs us of the world's problems. But it is hard to find a solution if we don't have a deep understanding of the problem, and only a book is capable of helping you understand it at the necessary level. Short publications will show you that there is a problem. A book will help you have a depth of understanding to be able to do something to solve it.
- Books develop your world-perspective. In a good book, the author takes the time and space to pass on to you his perspective on any given subject. That time and space allow you to learn new perspectives and expand your world-vision. In a good book, the author shares with you his thoughts and life experiences. Writing a book is a long and arduous task. Thus, the information at your disposal is invaluable to you.
- They increase your power of concentration. All day we are bombarded by hundreds of pieces of content that cause us to live

lives with a lack of concentration and vision. A book forces you develop again the muscle of concentration and focus.

- They develop your creative ability. The simple fact of reading a good fiction book will cause your mind to create scenarios, landscapes, and characters. This process of forcing your mind to imagine, will increase your creative and innovative skills.

2. The perfect moment to read will probably never come. So, read, at least a little every day.

Everyone has a busy life. Don't expect to find the perfect place to read. Simply read. Have a book handy all the time. If you are waiting for someone, read. If you are in the bathroom, read. If you are about to go to bed, read a couple of minutes before going to sleep. Take advantage of the small opportunities to read during the day. It's better to read two pages a day than not read at all for months just because you don't have time.

3. Read whatever you want. One basic key to build my love for reading was when one of my mentors told me you don't need to necessarily read what people recommend, read whatever you want.

If you go to a bookstore and a book captures you, buy it and read it. There is nothing more boring than reading a book that you feel obligated to read. Read what excites you. Remember that reading requires a much greater effort than watching TV or checking your Facebook account. So, make sure to read what you love. That will make your journey immensely easier.

4. Don't become obsessed with finishing a book. This was one of the best pieces of advice that I have received. If the author is good, you won't be able to leave it. If the author is so-so, he will lose his readers.

If I don't get captivated by a book in the first five chapters, I stop reading it and get another one. It is preferable to be constantly reading books that excite you and capture your attention than to stop reading for months because you committed to finishing a book that you lost interest in.

If you are reading this, it must be because this book seemed useful to you in some way. I hope you don't feel obligated to finish it, but rather you will continue to read it because it maintains your enthusiasm.

5. Use the book, draw lines in it, underline it, write notes in the margins, dog-ear the pages. Books are not to create a beautiful library at home in order to impress your visitors with everything you have read and your wisdom. It isn't necessary to take care of them as if they were collectable. Read, underline, dog-ear the pages, write on them, and what's more, if someday, we meet each other personally, I would love to see that you underlined and made notes, that the book was really used.

6. Add fiction books to your reading. I normally read non-fiction. I have always loved books about leadership and personal growth. But a while ago, I learned the power of adding fiction to my reading.

As I mentioned before, reading a good fiction book forces your mind to generate scenes, landscapes, and characters. It compels you to convert descriptions into real objects created by your mind. That power to create and imagine is like a muscle that you develop when you use it, and a good fiction book is the best exercise to build that capacity of being creative and imaginative.

7. Read with another person: your partner, friend, or group. Reading in a group, or with your partner, or a friend is excellent. On several occasions, my wife, friends, and I have chosen a book. We read it individually, and then we meet once a week to talk about it.

This process allowed me to learn new perspectives about the same subject, deepen my relationship, and keep myself motivated to keep reading. As I said in the chapter about community, having one is key to being successful in any area of your life, including reading.

8. Transfer to others the most important message of the book. The best way to learn and internalize a subject is by teaching others. When you read a book, a chapter, or even a phrase that had an impact on you, you need to pass it on to others. Teach others what you learned. That way, you will not only help others in their development, but you will influence them to get into the habit of reading.

9. Motivate others to read. I am always trying to motivate others to read. I am convinced of its benefits. When people ask me about a subject, what I do is recommend a book to them. I do it for the following reasons:

> That is my advice for your journey: Read, and never stop reading.
> #innerherobook.com

- A good book will give a more complete and better explanation than I can.
- A book requires commitment, and I want to know if the person is really interested in the answer, in growing and changing or is just asking for the sake of asking.
- If I make that person fall in love with reading, I know that I helped in deeply transforming that person.

10. Put into action what you've read. You can read entire libraries and present yourself before the world as the expert on any specific subject, but in the end, the important thing is how reading influenced your life for good. That's why you need to always put into action what you've read.

That is my advice for your journey: Read, and never stop reading.

PART SIX

FINAL WORDS

CHAPTER 22

FROM SUCCESS
TO SIGNIFICANCE

IN 2000, BILL GATES DECIDED to resign as CEO at Microsoft, a company he had founded twenty years earlier that made him the richest man in the world for more than five years.

Back in 1975, Bill Gates along with his partner Paul Allen founded Microsoft, a software company for personal computers born with the vision that every home would have a personal computer. A vision that even though it sounds logical at this time of history was not credible at the time that Bill and Paul decided to found their company.

During the next three decades, Microsoft led the software market for personal computers and revolutionized the tech world with the launch of Windows, Office, and, some years later, Xbox—the video console created to dominate every room of every house around the world.

The success of Microsoft made Bill Gates the richest man in the world in 1995 and kept him in first place practically until today, with the exception of 2008 to 2010, and again in 2013 when he was overtaken by Warren Buffett and Carlos Slim. At the time of this writing, Bill Gates's fortune is estimated at more than eighty billion dollars.

So then why did Bill Gates resign back in 2000 from the company that had been his dream and had made him the richest man in the entire world? Why did Bill Gates demote himself in the company and some months later announce he was going to shorten his work hours to devote himself to something else? Why was he walking away when he was at the top of success?

> A hero devotes his life to a greater cause than his treasure.
> #innerherobook.com

Was he possibly receiving a new call to adventure? Was he starting a new hero's journey? What was calling him?

Throughout this book I have described the hero as the person who wants something and is willing to go through conflict to get it. Right now, I want to give more detail about the real meaning. After reading multiple books and documents about the word *hero* I came to a conclusion. This word means "the one who protects and serves." In other words, a hero can become a hero if he devotes his life to a greater cause than his treasure. A hero needs to devote his or her life to a cause that is good and protects others.

A hero has three characteristics:

> A hero is a different person, more mature and with a stronger character at the end of the journey.
> #innerherobook.com

1. **Growth.** A hero goes through an evolution and growth process along the journey, such as we learned in the chapter on conflict and victory. A hero is a different person, more mature and with a stronger character at the end of the journey.

2. **Action.** A hero takes action, not just thinks about it. Like I said

before, in a movie the character's intentions can't be communicated, just the actions. If the director wants to communicate that a character is generous, he or she has to perform an act of generosity in the movie in order to be understood by the audience. A hero is like that in real life; a hero understands that it is not intentions, but actions that makes him or her a hero.

> A hero understands that it is not intentions, but actions that makes him or her a hero.
> #innerherobook.com

3. **Sacrifice.** A hero understands that he has to put something valuable aside, including his own dreams or even his own life, for an ideal or common good, for the purpose of taking mankind to a better place.

Nobody gets inspired by a story of a hero that struggles all his life for a selfish goal. Nobody wants to watch a movie about a person that devoted years to working, and went through hundreds of conflicts, to be able to buy a BMW.

There is nothing wrong with wanting or having a BMW, but in the end, that is a personal goal, it isn't the treasure that inspires and takes mankind to a better place. People get inspired by heroes that sacrifice themselves for the good of all, by heroes who understand what it means to be a hero, to protect and serve.

Rob Bell says that we need to try to find suffering in the world and do something about it, otherwise, we become miserable.

There is something wonderful about people who devote their lives doing something for others. It's as if heaven finally gave you the name hero.

Could this be what happened to Bill Gates? Could this be the reason that he was leaving his dream behind and the company that made him the richest man in the world? Was he consciously or unconsciously looking to become a real hero?

In 2000, Bill and his wife Melinda founded the Bill & Melinda Gates Foundation, a non-profit organization with the purpose of taking care of complicated worldwide issues like extreme poverty, health deficiency in developing countries, and correcting deficiencies in the American educational system.[1]

Bill gates abandoned his dream for a new one—a greater one than creating the best software or the best video game console, a dream that heals, that saves lives, and moves a country to further development.

Among the achievements of his foundation is the investment of more than ten billion dollars for research, the creation and delivery of vaccines to the neediest countries in the world, investments of more than five billion dollars to help eradicate polio by 2018 (India has already been declared polio-free.), and donation of more than one billion dollars for university scholarships in the next twenty years.

The Bill and Melinda Gates foundation has had such an impact that Warren Buffett, the second richest man in the world, decided to donate more than thirty billion dollars to the foundation in 2006. This is one of the greatest donations in history.

The point here is that the story of Bill Gates is inspiring not for the fact that he become the richest man in the world, but because he went on to became a man who is devoting his life and fortune to eradicate the most complex diseases on the planet, and helping poor countries to develop and correct the deficiencies in the American education system as well as others.

Do you want to become a real hero? Then you need to adjust your dreams and goals (your treasure) in order to help mankind some way. Only in this way will you be able to live a story that is worth living and telling.

A lot of people believe that the only option is to put aside your dreams and move to Africa to feed the needy. And, although I believe that could be a good choice for some, I also believe that both you and I can find a way to adapt our day- to-day, our dreams, and our goals to do good for others while we walk out our journeys.

I will never forget that meeting at Procter & Gamble with the then President of P&G Venezuela, Edward Jardine. As a team, we were proposing a last-minute opportunity in which we needed a huge investment in order to have a product ready for one of our clients. That meant a good boost for our sales, but a blow to our margin of profit due to how much we had to pay at the last minute in order to have the product ready.

Edward Jardine wasn't very pleased with the idea of affecting our profit margin and jeopardizing the organization for the sake of a rush-job to supply this specific need of a client, who had become used to rushing us because of their lack of efficiency in the planning process.

However, there was something in Jardine's heart that committed him to use his immense influence as the head of such a huge organization to do good for mankind. In that moment Jardine said:

"Ok. I am willing to invest in the product but only if you hire people with Down's syndrome to work in the production line."

"What? I don't believe that we will be able to have the product ready on time if we do it that way," the manager of logistics responded.

"Well, hire more people," was Jardine's answer. "If you want to supply the product for the event, I will approve it only if we give the opportunity to people with Down's syndrome. That is the only way I will approve it. Period."

And that is how it was done.

He wanted to use his influence and power to do good for mankind. You and I can do that every day with our work, our business, and other activities. We need to devote ourselves to people; we need to give our lives to take mankind to a better place.

That will turn you into a real hero.

> The hero's journey will only make sense if your treasure is for the benefit of mankind. That is the only way.
>
> #innerherobook.com

Remember this, the hero's journey will only make sense if your treasure is for the benefit of mankind. That is the only way.

When you devote yourself to others you start really building a legacy in the minds and hearts of others. As I heard Scott Mautz, an executive of Procter & Gamble, say one time: When you create a legacy, you beat death. When you die, you never really die, you just divide yourself into thousands of pieces that live in the hearts of all of those you touched during your life.

Decide to be everlasting. Decide to live forever in the heart of thousands of people. Decide to be the real hero. That is the only way you will move forward from success to significance.

CHAPTER 23

THE BIRTH OF A MOVEMENT

THE WORLD NEEDS YOU. The world needs to see and listen to your story.

Allow me in closing, to tell you about my dream.

This book is the result of hundreds of hours of work, a lot of sweat, and more than one tear. In order to write these lines I completely focused and tried to give everything that's in my heart in order to show you the hero's journey and motivate you to plunge into the adventure of your life. One of my greatest wishes is that you live a life worth living and telling.

But my dream is even bigger. It's not only about you, but what you can do for others.

My dream is to create a movement, a legion of heroes, and I need your help to make it come true.

Don't keep this book to yourself. Everything you've just read and learned will be very helpful to many people that haven't understood the

> My dream is to create a movement, a legion of heroes, and I need your help to make it come true.
> #innerherobook.com

purpose of their lives, that are afraid to plunge into the pursuit of their dreams and are in the middle of the ordeal with no understanding of the reason why they are trapped in the comfort of their ordinary world.

There are millions of people living neutralized and boring lives, people who, if someone were to make a movie about their lives, would make them confront a sad reality, people walking day after day toward their graves with their unsung song still within them.

The very same reason for writing this book, of waking them up to live their lives to the fullest, is now in your hands.

This book can't remain with you.

Give it to someone who needs it. If you feel that it's yours because it's full of notes, then buy another copy to give to your loved one. Learn the hero's journey and teach it to others.

In the same way I motivated you to become a hero, I encourage you now to become a mentor.

Can you imagine if all of your work team was a legion of heroes? How would it be if your family understood the concept of the hero's journey and were fighting every day for their treasure? What would the world be like if people understood that being a hero means sacrificing for and helping mankind get to a better place? How many people do you know that are in the middle of an ordeal and would be benefited by reading the chapters on conflict here within this book?

Help me share the message, help me spread the word.

Today, I want to invite you to become a part of this movement whose goal is not only to help you live a great story, but to teach and motivate others to do the same.

Let's help others to awaken their inner hero.

I thought for a long time about how to close this chapter, the most important one of this book, the final chapter. After a lot of thinking, I decided to finish it up with the following: Thank you! Thank you, for reading these words I wrote with great effort and out of love for you. I hope to have written what you were expecting. I hope to have helped you along the journey that is your life. That would be the best gift I could receive. With all my heart, thank you very, very much!

I ask God that we one day might meet each other personally, and you can tell me your story. I want to listen to it, to learn about your dreams, your passion, and your treasure. I would like you to tell me about your fears and how you overcame them. I also know that we will have a deep conversation about the ordeal that you went through. I want to listen to how you are helping mankind get to a better place. I want to be impacted and inspired by your story.

I want to look you in your eyes and say, "Congratulations! you are the hero of your life. Thank you for inspiring mine."

Remember that one day, when we depart from this world, your life will pass before your eyes…

…so make sure that it is something worth watching.

Remember that one day, when we depart from this world, your life will pass before your eyes…
…so make sure that it is something worth watching.
#innerherobook.com

CONTACT

Would you like to contact me?
I would love to hear your story.

Please visit:
www.revolutionigniter.com

You can also follow me on Twitter at @vhmanzanilla
Don't forget to tell me your story!

NOTES

Chapter 1

1. Donald Miller, *Million Miles in a Thousand Years* (Nashville: Thomas Nelson, 2009), 24–25.
2. Phrase wrongfully attributed to Henry David Thoreau. For more information, see "The Henry D. Thoreau Mis-Quotation Page," The Walden Woods Project, https://www.walden.org/thoreau/mis-quotations/.

Chapter 2

1. *Braveheart*, DVD, directed by Mel Gibson (1995; [Hollywood, CA]: Paramount Home Video, 2002).
2. Steven Pressfield, *The War of Art* (New York: Black Irish Books, 2013), 49.
3. John Eldredge, *Wild at Heart* (Nashville: Thomas Nelson, 2001).

Chapter 3

1. Joseph Campbell, *The Hero with a Thousand Faces* (Princeton: Princeton University Press, 1972).
2. Christopher Vogler, *The Writer's Journey* (Studio City, CA: Michael Wiese Productions, 2007).

Chapter 4

1. *The Shawshank Redemption*, DVD, directed by Frank Darabont (1994; [Burbank, CA]: Warner Home Video, 1999).

Chapter 5

1. "Founder, Scott Harrison, explains charity: water's Role in Solving the Water Crisis," Scott Harrison, 2013 Inbound Conference, http://www.charitywater.org/about/scotts_story.php.
2. Ibid.

3. "Best of Curtis Martin Hall of Fame Speech," the website of the NFL, http://www.nfl.com/videos/nfl-hall-of-fame/0ap2000000046274.

4. "Discovering Your Passion Is to Turn On Your Light," the website of Marco Ayuso, February 19, 2014 http://marcoayuso.com/descubrir-tu-pasion-es -encender-tu-luz.

Chapter 6

1. See John Goddard, "Another Brand on the List," in Chicken Soup for the Soul, eds. Jack Canfield and Mark Victor Hansen (Deerfield Beach, FL: Health Communications, 1993).

2. John Goddard, *The Survivor: 24 Spine-Chilling Adventures on the Edge of Death* (Deerfield Beach, FL: Health Communications, 2001).

3. "John Goddard – Dateline NBC," interview available at http://www. johngoddard.info/.

4. "Starbucks CEO Howard Schultz Talking about His Return as CEO," website for unofficial Starbucks news and culture, June 30, 2011, http://starbucksmelody.com/2011/06/30/ starbucks-ceo-howard-schultz -talking-about-his -return-as-ceo/.

Chapter 7

1. Robert McKee, *Story: Style, Structure, Substance, and the Principles of Screenwriting,* (New York: ReganBooks, 1997).

2. *The Hobbit*, DVD, directed by Peter Jackson (2012; [Hollywood, CA]: Warner Brothers Pictures, 2013).

3. J. R. R.Tolkien, *The Hobbit* (Boston: Houghton Mifflin, 1966).

4. Pressfield, *War of Art.*

5. Charles Duhigg, *The Power of Habit* (New York: Random House, 2012), 109–111.

6. Roald Amundsen, *The South Pole*, vol. 1 (New York: Lee Keedick, 1913), 370.

Chapter 8

1. *The Way*, DVD, directed by Emilio Estevez (2010; [Santa Monica, CA]: Arc Entertainment, 2012.)

2. Ibid.

3. Miller, *A Million Miles*, 113–14.

4. Ibid., pp. 130–31.

5. Ibid., 160.

6. Tolkien, *The Hobbit*, 64.

7. Pressfield, *War of Art*, 19.

Chapter 9

1. Pressfield, *War of Art*, 18, 73, 75.

Chapter 10

1. "Tony's Biography," the Tony Melendez website, ttp://www.tonymelendez
   .com/English/Welcome.html
2. Rob Bell, "Drops Like Stars," conference in Columbus, Ohio, 2010.
3. Ibid.
4. Miller, *A Million Miles*, 188.
5. John Maxwell, Leadership Conference, Mexico City, 2014.
6. Elisabeth Kubler-Ross, Death: The Final Stage of Growth (New York: Simon & Schuster, 1975), 96.
7. "What Michelangelo Can Teach You About Good Design," Chanpory Rith, January 29, 2008, http://www.lifeclever.com/what-michelangelo-can -teach-you-about-good-design.

Chapter 11

1. ErikWeihenmayer, Latinnovation Conference, Cincinnati, Ohio, 2007.
2. John Maxwell, Leadership Conference, Mexico City, 2014.
3. Malcolm Gladwell, Outliers (New York: Little Brown and Company, 2008).
4. Daniel Levitin, This Is Your Brain on Music (NewYork: Penguin, 2006), 197.

Chapter 12

1. Michael Jordan, I Can't Accept Not Trying (San Francisco: HarperSanFrancisco, 1994).
2. Pressfield, *War of Art*, 45.
3. "'Never Ever Give Up:' Diana Nyad Completes Historic Cuba-to-Florida Swim," Matt Sloane, Jason Hanna, and Dana Ford, CNN, September 3, 2013, http://www.cnn.com/2013/09/02/world /americas /diana-nyad-cuba-florida-swim/.
4. "Citizenship in a Republic," Theodore Roosevelt, speech delivered at the Sorbonne, Paris, France, April 23, 1019, http://design.caltech.edu/erik /Misc/Citizenship_in_a_Republic.pdf

Chapter 13

1. Miller, *A Million Miles*, 182.
2. Vogler. *The Writer's Journey*, 54.
3. Robin Pogrebin, "From Waitress to Brother's Savior, Then Hollywood Hero," *The New York Times*, October 12, 2010, http://www.nytimes .com/2010/10/13/movies/13waitress.html.
4. Ibid.
4. Pressfield, *The War of Art,* 179.

Chapter 16

1. Rudy, DVD, directed by David Anspaugh (1993; [Culver City, CA]: Sony Pictures Home Entertainment, 2008).

Chapter 18

1. Greg McKeown, *Essentialism: The Disciplined Pursuit of Less.* (New York: Crown Business, 2014).
2. "CEO 101: Legendary Costco Leader Talks Business with UW-Greenbay Students," Christopher Samson, "Inside UW-Greenbay News," April 3, 2014, http:// news.uwgb.edu/featured/leading-learning/04/03 /sinegal-costco-leader-talks-to-students.

Chapter 19

1. "Gene Weingarten: Setting the Record Straight on the Joshua Bell Experiment," *The Washington Post,* October 14, 2014, http://www.washingtonpost.com/news/style/wp/2014/10/14/gene -weingarten- setting-the-record-straight-on-the-joshua-bell-experiment.
2. "Intensely Alive," Facundo Cabral March 13, 2008, http://www .facundocabral.info/literatura-texto.php?Id=83.

Chapter 20

1. "The Habit," from Natalie Conrad "A Poem: 'The Habit,'" http://www .organizedhabits.com/a-poem.

Chapter 22

1. "Who We Are, History," Bill and Melinda Gates Foundation, http://www .gatesfoundation.org/Who-We-Are/General-Information/History.

BIBLIOGRAPHY

Campbell, Joseph. The Hero with a Thousand Faces. Princeton, NJ: Princeton University Press, 1972.

Canfield, Jack and MarkVictor Hanses. *Chicken Soup for the Soul*. Deerfield Beach, FL: Health Communications, 1995.

Duhigg, Charles. *The Power of Habit*. Barcelona: Urano, 2015.

Edgredge, John. Wild at Heart. Nashville: Thomas Nelson, 2001.

Gladwell, Maxwell. Outliers. New York: Little Brown and Company, 2008.

Jordan, Michael. I Can't Accept Not Trying. San Francisco: HarperSanFrancisco, 1994.

Levitin, Daniel. This Is Your Brain on Music: The Science of a Human Obsession. New York: Dutton, 2006.

McKee, Robert. Story: Substance, Structure, Style and the Principles of Screenwriting. New York: ReganBooks, 1997.

McKeown, Greg. Essentialism: The Disciplined Pursuit of Less. New York: Crown Business, 2014.

Miller, Donald. *A Million Miles in a Thousand Years*. Nashville: Thomas Nelson, 2009.

Pressfield, Steven. *The War of Art*. New York: Black Irish Books, 2013.

Tolkien, J. R. R. *The hobbit*. Barcelona: Minotauro, 1982.

Vogler, Christopher. The Writer's Journey. Studio City, CA: Michael Wiese Productions, 2007.

ABOUT THE AUTHOR

VICTOR HUGO MANZANILLA is a marketing manager with more than fifteen years of experience in the creation of multi-million-dollar brands in Fortune 500 companies and the development of high-performance work teams. His passion for leadership, management, entrepreneurship, and personal development brought him to establish LiderazgoHoy.com, a blog and podcast visited by more than one million people every year. Victor Hugo has positioned himself as one of the main leaders of thought in the field and is internationally recognized as one of the most inspiring speakers of today. He resides with his family in Florida.